THE MILITARY MODELLER'S COMPENDIUM

THE MILITARY MODELLER'S COMPENDIUM

Ken Jones

ARGUS BOOKS

Argus Books
Argus House
Boundary Way
Hemel Hempstead
Herts HP2 7ST
England

First published by Argus Books 1992

ISBN 1 85486 053 4

Phototypesetting by Photoprint
Printed and bound in Great Britain by
William Clowes Ltd., Beccles.

CONTENTS

THE MILITARY MODELLER'S COMPENDIUM

INTRODUCTION

Reader response to the publication of my first Military Modelling title, *A Guide to Military Modelling* in 1987, was very favourable. Many readers, some known to me, but the majority unknown, kindly took the trouble to compliment me on a comprehensive little book for beginners. Some also took the opportunity to offer constructive criticism for which I am always very grateful.

An important 'criticism' was that the book did not go far enough in its illustrative content and I have since been constantly urged to put this right. It is obvious that pictures mean a lot to modellers and so the idea for expanding and enlarging the book whilst updating the text where necessary was considered by the publisher.

Little could be added to the original text, save for taking the opportunity to update it in certain areas and to enlarge the appendix with more addresses. It was, after all, originally based on a lot of feedback gained from the hundreds of queries that I, as editor of *Military Modelling*

magazine, have received over the years. Because a lot of our readers, especially those new to the hobby, usually asked the same questions, the first little book became a reality.

This time around, however, colour pictures have been specially prepared, along with a full complement of illustrations replacing all those in the original book. All step-by-step sequences were taken especially for this book's new and enlarged format and I've focused on those areas I know to be of special interest for beginners to the hobby. For example, painting the face of a miniature figurine and also horses are high on beginners' request lists.

It's customary to dedicate books these days . . . I'd like to dedicate this one to the readers of *Military Modelling* magazine past and present, because without them there would be no hobby at all!

Ken Jones
Leighton Buzzard
1992

CHAPTER 1

SCALES AND THE MILITARY MODELLER

An understanding of scales is essential in any modelling pursuit, and a good working knowledge is essential if you are to understand the mass of unfamiliar data found on packaging, which can often confuse the modelling beginner.

Unfortunately, there is very little standardisation on scales, either by manufacturers or the model press. It is quite common to see a scale quoted as a ratio, a mixture of metric and imperial measure and a 'borrowed' coding system from railway modelling: thus, 1:76; 4mm = 1 foot; OO/HO.

So far as the military modeller is concerned, there are two situations where scales apply – figure and vehicle modelling – and these become important when entering models in competitions or when a collection of figures or vehicles, or both together in diorama form, is envisaged. In order to simplify matters somewhat, I will explain figure scales and vehicle scales separately but, where they are compatible, I will indicate this.

Commercial availability also dictates popularity, and segregation of models into various so-called 'popular scales' is common practice simply because much use can be made of kit parts. Any further additions or new ranges are, therefore, designed to these 'popular scales', particularly in the case of plastic model vehicle kits. However, figures, while following nominal scales, do diverge into many unusual and, in many cases, 'one-off' sizes, but seemingly more by accident than design. Before listing the scales used in military modelling, a basic explanation is necessary.

RATIOS

Scales are expressed as ratios for both figures and model vehicle kits, but mainly for the latter. The ratio is simply an expression of relative size. For example, 1:35 means that the model is $\frac{1}{35}$th the size of the real thing – one inch or one millimetre on the model is 35 inches or 35 millimetres on the real thing. Thus, if the model is one foot or one metre long, the subject from which it is taken is 35 feet or 35 metres long. No matter which way it is expressed, or which 'units' are used for measuring, one unit on the model will still be represented by 35 on the real thing.

Once this is fully understood, scales are easily worked out on your pocket calculator. Modellers' plans are still published which quote a ratio and have a bar scale in feet, and sometimes a dual feet/metres scale is included. Modellers 'brought up' with imperial measure do not always feel comfortable with metric measure and often convert freely between the two, which gives rise to manufacturers labelling some model kits, for example, 4mm = 1 foot, or 1:76 scale.

This is derived from converting the ratio thus:

$$\frac{1 \times 25.4 \times 12}{76} = 4\text{mm represents one foot}$$

25.4 is the conversion factor for inches to millimetres.

Try working out examples of different ratios until it becomes second nature and you are fully conversant with the equation. Thereafter, checking figures and kit parts will become easier.

Nominal dimensions

Heights in millimetres are the most commonly quoted model figure scales and are freely referred to as such by modellers. Ratios, for obvious reasons, are used for vehicles, although they can also be used for figures.

Figure heights were expressed in inches many years ago, but are now exclusively quoted in millimetres. The model figure is measured from the ground to the top of the head, *excluding* head-dress, not, as is sometimes erroneously quoted, from the ground to eye level. Simply measure model figure heights just as we measure our own

Military Modelling scale rule being used to check a 75mm Clydecast British infantryman c. 1815.

– from the ground to the top of the head.

The most common or traditional military model figurine size is 54mm (2 inches) which is also sometimes referred to as 1:32 scale. Figures in this scale are often referred to colloquially by modellers as 'fifty-fours'.

The height of any figurine is usually calculated on a 'human form' of 5 feet 9 inches tall (1.75 metres) which is adopted as an average height. Obviously human heights and statures vary, but rarely do designers 'adjust' their model figures accordingly.

Figures in the larger scales, which are normally plastic construction kits, though there are some large-scale polyurethane resin figure kits available, are indicated as ratios rather than nominal height, e.g. 1:9 and 1:12 scales. A list of common scales in use, along with product availability plus a table of ratios, 1:1 to 1:100, are appended at the end of this chapter.

Other designations

Vehicles and figures in the smaller scales can bear the dimensional description more associated with model railways. These are 00 (1:76 scale) and HO (1:87 scale). Often the two are incorrectly lumped together as OO/HO to add further to the confusion.

The origin of this unfortunate merger can be traced back some 60 years and resulted from British model railway manufacturers' design faults in rounding everything up, above the wheels, of the Continental and US gauge of 16.5mm or HO where 1 foot equalled 3.5mm, so that 4mm equalled 1 foot. If 1:76 scale was to be used, then the track gauge should have been 18.8mm against 16.5mm. For example a British model locomotive would have its body in 1:76 scale and its wheels and the trackwork to 1:87 scale! Although there are 1:76 and 1:87 scale military vehicles, the British manufacturer Airfix still insisted on labelling its kits OO/HO,

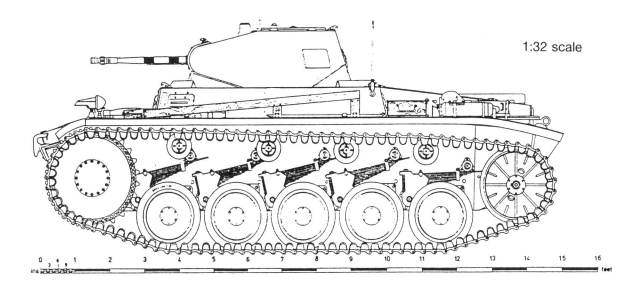

1:32 scale

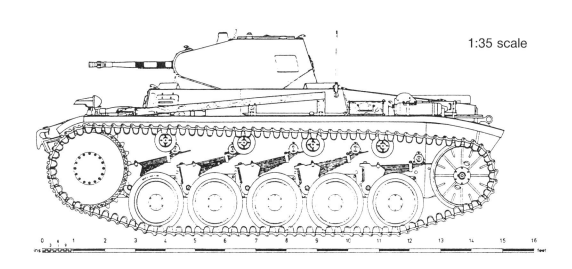

1:35 scale

1:76 scale

1:87 scale

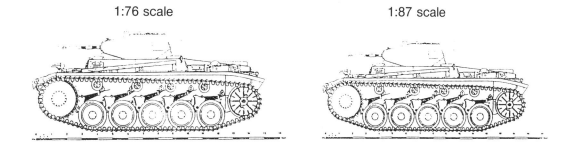

Side elevations of a *PzKpfw II* to show the differences in size for four popular scales. There is an appreciable difference between 1:32 scale and the now most popular scale of 1:35.

which is wrong! There is a marked visual and dimensional difference from placing a 1:87 scale AFV against the same type in 1:76 scale.

The table provides a list of the commoner scales the military modeller will encounter.

SCALES, SPACE AND COLLECTING

When most people take up modelling of any sort, they do not, as a rule, adhere to any common scale. When they become more experienced in the hobby, specialising in one particular scale becomes the norm.

The scale, or scales, a modeller adopts is often dictated by the immediate domestic environment. Big armoured vehicles, lorries and figures around 100mm tall take up a lot of storage space, and no one really likes to have the fruits of their labours hidden away in boxes in the attic when they should be on display.

Selecting an 'ideal' scale is purely a personal choice, but it is worth considering any prohibiting factors that may emerge as you progress. While it's a good idea – and good practice – to try your hand at painting different sizes of figurines, for example, you should bear in mind where you will keep them all and whether you have sufficient display and storage space. Models can be displayed on a rota system – some on display and some in storage. This is what museums do to ensure their full collections are displayed over a period of time in the space available.

Popular scales

Although you can make models to any size, scales are usually dictated by commercial output and availability. The following are some of the most popular.

1:87 scale A popular scale in continental Europe, equating to a figure height of 20mm and often labelled as 'HO', which is the model railway scale. HO means simply 'half 'O' Gauge', which was the popular model railway scale in the United Kingdom and on the Continent of 7mm = 1 foot.

Model vehicle availability, including figures, is very good from Roco Minitanks, Faller and Preiser plus the huge Wiking range of mainly commercial vehicles. As always, confusion occurs and some British manufacturers list 20mm figures as 1:76 scale which is not surprising when one considers the British 'manufacturing approach' to railway scales and gauges.

1:76 scale Popularised by Airfix in the early 1960s and based on the British model railway scale of OO or, as often labelled, '4mm = 1 foot scale'. This is a scale rigidly adhered to by some British AFV scratchbuilders for whom its popularity is promoted and kept alive. Figures should scale out at around 23mm plus. Plenty of military vehicle kits are available to this scale, though the 'boom' period has passed.

It is a good scale for scratchbuilders and for large collections and the space-conscious. Figure modellers will find the size a 'little too small', although some do collect and convert plastic commercial figures in this scale.

1:72 scale The most popular model aircraft scale. A large variety of figures and vehicle kits is widely available, mainly from Japan, although Italian manufacturers have added many more. Some well-detailed figures intended for wargames moulded in soft, polythene-type plastic available from Revell and ESCI are most attractive to collectors.

1:58 scale An unfamiliar ratio, but one that equates to the figure height of 30mm, and a scale once popular with figure painters but which has now limited appeal. Phoenix Model Developments, Tradition and others did produce 30mm figures and these still may be found. The scale was popular for displaying military bands in their entirety. Vehicles are not available in great numbers.

1:48 scale   Also known as 'quarter scale' and another popular model aircraft scale. There are not as many model vehicle kits in this scale as there were around 20 years ago, but recent figure and vehicle kit releases from the Belgian manufacturer, Verlinden, have somewhat redressed this state of affairs. Figures are mainly produced for aircraft ground crews, aircrew and the like. Figures in this scale are around 37mm high.

1:43 scale   Not much, if anything, in the way of vehicle construction kits in this scale, which has been adopted by collectors of die-cast models, Dinky Toys, etc. The French company, Solido, still produce some tanks and military vehicles in 1:43 scale. Also listed as 7mm scale or O gauge model railway scale, the figures are around 40mm tall and military types are not available in any quantity or variety.

1:35 scale   The most popular military vehicle kit scale introduced during the early 1960s with imports from Japan. Figures are available from the major plastic kit manufacturers and notably from the British manufacturers Hornet and Lead Sled and the Belgian companies of Verlinden and Belgo. Limited to the WWII period to the present day, the figures are around 50-52mm tall and are designed to accompany vehicles in dioramas or displayed as single figures.

A very good choice of vehicle kits of all periods plus resin and white metal figure ranges are constantly added to by British, Belgian, German, French, US, Italian and, of course, Japanese manufacturers.

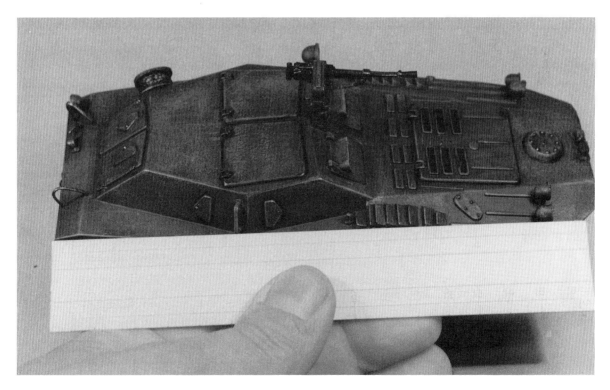

Military Modelling scale rule in use checking the basic dimensions of a 1:35 scale Soviet BRDM armoured car.

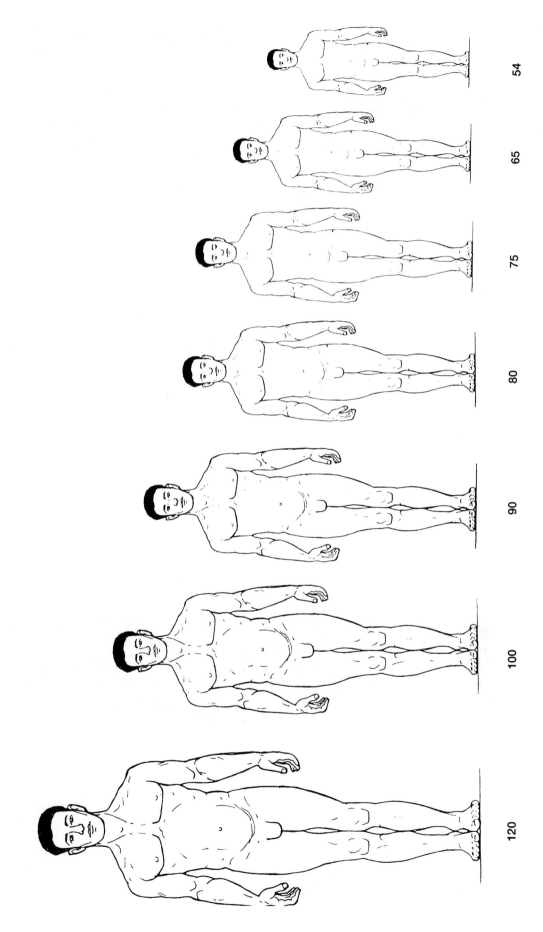

54

65

75

80

90

100

120

Popular figure heights from 120mm to 54mm represented diagrammatically.

1:32 scale A very popular model figure scale which is more commonly referred to as 54mm scale, being the nominal height of the model figurines. Vehicles to this scale are nowhere as numerous as 1:35 scale. Airfix 'flirted' with making vehicles in this scale, and very good they were too! There are some white metal construction kits of vehicles from Scale Link of WWI designs. Quite a number of aircraft kits are produced in this scale too.

There are more figures produced in 54mm scale than any other as practically every figure manufacturer produces models in this scale offering plenty of choice.

1:30 scale The vehicle scale adopted by some Russian and Eastern countries for plastic kits which are available only in limited numbers in the West. This scale, around 58mm tall, is also the size adopted by Historex of Paris for their plastic figure models – mainly all subjects of the Napoleonic wars period. *Note:* Some white metal figures are produced to 60mm and 65mm scales, probably more from 'over-estimation' on a 54mm figure by the sculptor than by design! However, 65mm scale seems to have established itself with some manufacturers, and will, therefore, probably become accepted and standardised.

1:24 scale The nominal 75mm figure scale, also termed half-inch scale. Closely allied to 1:25 scale for vehicles and some plastic figures from Japanese manufacturers. Good variety in 75mm white metal figures mainly from British figure designers.

1:20 scale Not many vehicles in this scale, but plenty of figures where 87mm equals the height of a 5 feet 9 inches' tall person, although this 'rounds' off to 90mm plus, a very popular larger figure scale.

1:15 scale A newly introduced approxi-

mate scale of polyurethane resin figure kits, 120mm high from the Belgian manufacturer Verlinden Productions and called 'Super Scale'. Other manufacturers have followed suit and are producing figures, mainly resin, in this scale.

Larger scales Some plastic figure construction kits, from Airfix, Tamiya and Imai to 1:12 scale and ESCI in 1:9 scale are eagerly sought, built and converted by modellers. These are plastic, injection-moulded kits of a hollow construction and thus easy to convert, especially by beginners. The figures are ideal on which to practise conversions, once you have become adept at building them. Verlinden has released a 200mm 'Giant' scale figure which equates to around 1:9 scale.

Give plenty of thought and attention to scales, what they mean and why we use them. Learn and understand scales, as in the next chapter the use of drawings will be discussed. You will then not be deterred from building, say, a military vehicle in 1:35 scale when the only drawing you have available is to 1:40 scale and you know how to convert the dimensions.

Ratio	Nominal figure height in mm. Based on average equalling 5ft 9ins	Metric/ Imperial Millimetres equalling 1 foot	Remarks
1:300	6	1	Z Gauge (railway)
1:250	7	1.2	
1:200	9	1.5	
1:150	11.5	2	N Gauge (railway)
1:100	17.25	3	TT Gauge (Table Top railways)
1:96	18	3.2	
1:90	19	3.4	
1:87	20	3.5	HO Gauge (half O Gauge railway)
1:76	23	4	OO Gauge (railway – British)
1:72	24	4.2	
1:58	30	5	
1:50	34.5	6	
1:48	36.5	6.3	'Quarter Scale'
1:43	40	7	O Gauge (railway) International Die Cast Scale, (Solido tanks)

Ratio	Nominal figure height in mm. Based on average 5ft 9ins	Metric/ Imperial Millimetres equalling 1 foot	Remarks
1:40	44	7.6	
1:38	46	8	
1:35	50	8.7	The most popular AFV scale
1:32	54.5	9.5	
1:30	58	10	60mm nominal – Historex figures
1:25	69.5	12	
1:24	73	12.7	75mm nominal figure size
1:21	83	14.5	80mm nominal figure size
1:20	87	15.2	90mm nominal figure size
1:17	102	17.9	100mm nominal figure size
1:16	109.25	19	
1:15	116.7	20.3	120mm nominal figure size
1:10	175	30	
1:9	195	34	200mm nominal figure size
1:8	219	38	

(*Note:* Figures in metric/millimetres conversion and figure heights are rounded off for convenience.)

In the following table I've listed the ratios 1:1 through to 1:100 with scale dimensions in millimetres for feet and metres. I've mixed imperial and metric standards because modellers tend to think in feet and inches for the heights of humans, especially in the United Kingdom and the USA, and apply this to figurines. But for model vehicles and equipment, millimetres are used for convenience. I have listed the dimensions to two decimal places being within the limits the modeller can measure and cut to. The table is intended as a 'ready reckoner' for modellers to refer to, showing how many millimetres equal one foot or one metre in each particular ratio. You can work out any dimensions with your pocket calculator.

Ratio	mm = foot	mm = metre	Ratio	mm = foot	mm = metre	Ratio	mm = foot	mm = metre
1:1	304.8	1,000	1:34	8.96	29.4	1:67	4.54	14.9
1:2	152.4	500	1:35	8.70	28.5	1:68	4.48	14.7
1:3	101.5	333.3	1:36	8.46	27.7	1:69	4.41	14.4
1:4	76.2	250	1:37	8.23	27	1:70	4.35	14.2
1:5	60.96	200	1:38	8.02	26.3	1:71	4.29	14
1:6	50.79	166.6	1:39	7.81	25.6	1:72	4.23	13.8
1:7	43.54	142.8	1:40	7.62	25	1:73	4.17	13.6
1:8	38.1	125	1:41	7.43	24.3	1:74	4.11	13.5
1:9	33.86	111.1	1:42	7.25	23.8	1:75	4.06	13.3
1:10	30.48	100	1:43	7.08	23.2	1:76	4.01	13.1
1:11	27.7	90.9	1:44	6.92	22.7	1:77	3.95	12.9
1:12	25.39	83.3	1:45	6.77	22.2	1:78	3.9	12.8
1:13	23.4	76.9	1:46	6.62	21.7	1:79	3.85	12.6
1:14	21.7	71.4	1:47	6.48	21.2	1:80	3.81	12.5
1:15	20.31	66.6	1:48	6.34	20.8	1:81	3.76	12.3
1:16	19.05	62.5	1:49	6.22	20.4	1:82	3.71	12.1
1:17	17.92	58.8	1:50	6.09	20	1:83	3.67	12
1:18	16.93	55.5	1:51	5.97	19.6	1:84	3.62	11.9
1:19	16.04	52.6	1:52	5.86	19.2	1:85	3.58	11.7
1:20	15.24	50	1:53	5.75	18.8	1:86	3.54	11.6
1:21	14.51	47.6	1:54	5.64	18.5	1:87	3.5	11.4
1:22	13.85	45.4	1:55	5.54	18.1	1:88	3.46	11.3
1:23	13.25	43.4	1:56	5.44	17.8	1:89	3.42	11.2
1:24	12.69	41.6	1:57	5.34	17.5	1:90	3.38	11.1
1:25	12.19	40	1:58	5.25	17.2	1:91	3.34	10.9
1.26	11.72	38.4	1:59	5.16	16.9	1:92	3.31	10.8
1:27	11.28	37	1:60	5.07	16.6	1:93	3.27	10.7
1:28	10.88	35.7	1:61	4.99	16.3	1:94	3.24	10.6
1:29	10.51	34.4	1:62	4.91	16.1	1:95	3.2	10.5
1:30	10.15	33.3	1:63	4.83	15.8	1:96	3.17	10.4
1:31	9.83	32.2	1:64	4.76	15.6	1:97	3.14	10.3
1:32	9.52	31.2	1:65	4.68	15.3	1:98	3.11	10.2
1:33	9.23	30.3	1:66	4.61	15.1	1:99	3.07	10.1
						1:100	3.04	10

CHAPTER 2

RESEARCH AND THE MODELLER

Research work by modellers is just as interesting, and often more time-consuming, than actually painting a figure, building a tank kit or constructing a diorama. As modellers progress and their skills become more sharply honed, the search for perfection becomes paramount. Gone is the 'assemble, paint and display in a day' approach and building only what's supplied in the box; the modeller now aspires to getting it right. Whether this is adding detail or converting vehicles, changing or modifying uniform and equipment detail on figures, the urge to go that step further is very real.

Therefore, modellers need to find out as much as possible about the objects they model, in order to improve their standards and techniques in the quest for realism and accuracy. However, modelling is fun, so detailed research should always be taken in its correct context. Sadly, perhaps, modellers have been known to allow research to overtake their modelling pursuits and, in many cases, collecting research material can totally oust the basic initial pastime. Both aspects are good fun and, though research can become more mentally stimulating or frustrating, it should never be allowed to supersede the prime task of producing the model.

GATHERING MATERIAL

There is nothing more frustrating than to build, for example, a model vehicle and perpetuate a common mistake, incorporated by the manufacturer, which everyone else knows about except yourself! Basic research, and the most basic is verbal communication with fellow modellers, can avoid such errors. Alternatively, a visit to the local public library can often provide the information to ascertain any instructional or material mistakes. It should certainly put the researching modeller firmly on the right track and provide further references to check.

Be on the lookout for anything useful – not only material on current projects, but anything you consider worthwhile. Become a hoarder of everything pertaining to your hobby and remember two things: never throw anything away and, if you don't need it today, you are bound to want it tomorrow!

Museums

Military museums offer a wealth of information and they often have publications on sale of interest to the military modeller. Most larger towns and cities have regimental museums or similar establishments, in addition to the national museums in the capital and elsewhere. Visits to all such establishments should be encouraged whenever possible, after first making an appointment if necessary. Some military museums issue readers' tickets for researchers, so check before attending. Also, some are within military establishments where access is restricted. Conduct yourself correctly and remember that others may want to follow your line. One single unacceptable action could cause the withdrawal of facilities and ruin any chances of future research facilities for others.

The location of regimental museums can

usually be found in the local library. Often museums close for repairs, or are moved to different locations or, worse, closed down for good! The maintenance of a publication showing the location of all military museums in the United Kingdom or in the USA is not practical for publishers, but there have been books released giving a good core of information, most of which never really changes. See the Appendices for further details.

Official bodies in the UK

The United Kingdom Ministry of Defence (MoD) and foreign embassies are good sources of information. Public relations officers and military attachés are usually very helpful and responsive to reasonable requests, or can put you in touch with the appropriate contact who may be able to supply the relevant information. Remember, security does cover a good slice of military matters so do not expect information that is normally unavailable, particularly where equipment is concerned. However, uniforms and suchlike are subjects where information is readily made available.

Unlike museums, material from official bodies is normally supplied free of charge. The addresses of embassies (in the United Kingdom, for example, they are all in London) can be found in the telephone directory. It is surprising how many modellers ignore these excellent and often untapped sources of material.

Military shows and open days, also sources of prime material, should be visited whenever possible. A notebook and camera are essential on such visits and it is interesting to note how quickly you amass much useful information. Even the 'Cavalry Old Comrades' parade, a yearly event in London's Hyde Park, will offer much in the way of British army dress

uniforms; excellent reference for figure painters. You may not need the information gathered at the particular moment you obtain it, but you may in the future. Remember, what you get today will help tomorrow.

Libraries

Public libraries are fine institutions, coupled to the central library system operating in the UK. Virtually every book in print, and many of those out of print, can be obtained on application. Join your local library and use the facilities offered for research as an aid to your modelling.

Public records

Public records offices are useful when researching obscure information on military units and their uniforms, structure and so on. Access to records is usually by appointment at the office concerned, and it is wise to be specific in your requests so that the staff can give you maximum help. Know exactly what you are looking for and, before you begin, acquire as many leads as possible. You may have to wait a long time for research material to be delivered and, as in some records offices, readers' tickets may be necessary, check before you visit.

Press agencies

Good photographs and information can be obtained from newspaper offices and the many press agencies. Fees are charged – often expensive – by press agencies for private requests and this alone can deter the modeller with limited funds, but much excellent material is available from these sources. Foreign countries' press agencies are 'gold mines' to the diligent researcher. Advance appointments are required if you wish to go through records, and fees are normally charged for material.

Filing systems

It is a complete waste of your valuable time if you do not collate and store any information you acquire in a manner which will allow you to locate that information quickly.

The most obvious method of storing material is a scrapbook, or in some cases, a type of file card index. Written information is best put on a card system, and photographs and cuttings pasted into a scrapbook. Often the two can be used together and cross-referenced for ease of operation.

As a beginner, it is best that you start as you mean to continue. There is nothing worse than to have a lot of material jumbled up without any semblance of order which involves you having to spend a lot of time searching for what you want – or even to realise that you didn't really have what you're searching for in the first place! Always try to plan ahead.

A card index system is simple to begin and to maintain. Index cards are cheap and available in different sizes and should be stored alphabetically in boxes made specially for them, or in suitably sized card boxes. Smaller photographs can be stuck to index cards for a more compact system, but if larger magazine cuttings are to be stored they cannot really be incorporated in a standard card index system. These are better stuck into a scrapbook using a 'stick' type adhesive, such as Pritt, which is clean and non-staining.

Military modellers who paint figures or build vehicles need a lot of illustrative reference – uniform types, colour information, badges and the like, or close-up details of vehicles. If this is 'double-sided'

with material on both sides of a page removed from a magazine, store these in envelopes – unfolded – in manila folders or wallets, or in the transparent document wallets on sale in stationers.

As the reference material or library grows some form of index system will have to be devised.

With the growth in popularity of personal computer systems a whole new world of storing information electronically presents itself to modellers. Storage programs can be purchased or devised for accessing solid information or index purposes.

Cameras

Most people nowadays have a camera of some description. Modellers should try to use a camera whenever possible to accumulate as much pictorial reference as they can.

There are simple rules to follow when photographing for record purposes. If what you need to photograph is in a military museum, make sure that photography is permitted. Many museums do not allow the use of flash guns, so an appropriately high rated ASA/ISO film should be obtained before the visit. If you are at a show or military parade, ensure you do not obstruct anyone when obtaining your pictures. Also, do not photograph anything you are told not to. Such irresponsible actions can spoil things for everyone else.

Colour film processing is now much cheaper than black and white. In fact, black and white processing is expensive because of its labour intensive methods, but colour film and the colour values it gives should never be treated as exact references, only as a guide as explained in the next section on colour.

COLOUR AND THE MODELLER

The modeller must have some knowledge

about colour and what constitutes it. Figure modellers must know about the difference between 'red' and 'crimson', for instance, or between 'Prussian Blue' and 'French Blue'. Interpretation of colour is difficult, because we must reduce 'to scale' any paint colours we use, and experience is the only yardstick. It is no use trying to match colours to actual examples. Original sources can only be used as guidance – and guidance alone – for colour matching on any miniature subject.

Remember also that uniforms, especially old surviving examples, fade and so are not really reliable sources anyway. What it boils down to is that the modeller must use his or her own judgement. It is an indisputable fact that any two modellers will paint khaki in two different shades. The difference may be subtle, but different all the same.

This also holds true for vehicles. Fading and weathering all take their toll and, unless a 'factory finish' is desired, which never looks realistic in model form anyway, some measure of intelligent interpretation is needed.

Scale colour has been mentioned and this is simply the 'reduction' process making the colour appear lighter overall. You could not, for example, paint a model with the exact shade, or the same paint for that matter, as that used on the real thing. For a start, it would be too dark and this is where the colour has to be lightened and artistic licence taken – again experience will show what is right and what 'feels' and 'looks' right.

Colour pictures printed in magazines are not suitable for exact comparisons – a colour print or slide would be nearer but only if correctly exposed. Try altering your exposure on one subject and see what happens. You will be amazed at the difference the effects of light, reflected from say the green or olive drab of a tank, alters with camera aperture adjustments.

There are far too many myths surrounding so-called exact colour matching and a lot of rubbish talked about colour itself. If it looks right compared with the real thing then you've succeeded – if not, try again.

PLANS AND SCALE DRAWINGS

Unlike the figure modeller and painter, the vehicle modeller is a great user of plans of scale drawings. By the very nature of the subject – a tank, armoured car, truck, car or whatever – the modeller must at some time refer to a drawing or a photograph to improve upon the kit under construction. Later, when attempting a scratchbuilt model, a scale drawing is a necessity and, without it, making an accurate model would be virtually impossible.

Always follow one basic rule when working from drawings and that is to take measurements from the dimensions shown in all views – never from one view only. Also, observe how sloping surfaces are not equal in all views. This may sound obvious, but many people do make this most basic of errors, some repeatedly.

Drawing your own plans

It is almost impossible to teach anyone to produce scale drawings from a book. However, it is possible to pass on some pointers which should help anyone with a modicum of artistry to feel more confident about producing a drawing.

If you have access to the subject, a drawing is, of course, much easier. All basic measurements should be taken and, if the subject is large it helps to have an assistant. Photograph the subject from both sides, front and rear, and with as much detail as you consider necessary. Where possible, include a measuring rod marked off in feet or metres in the photo-

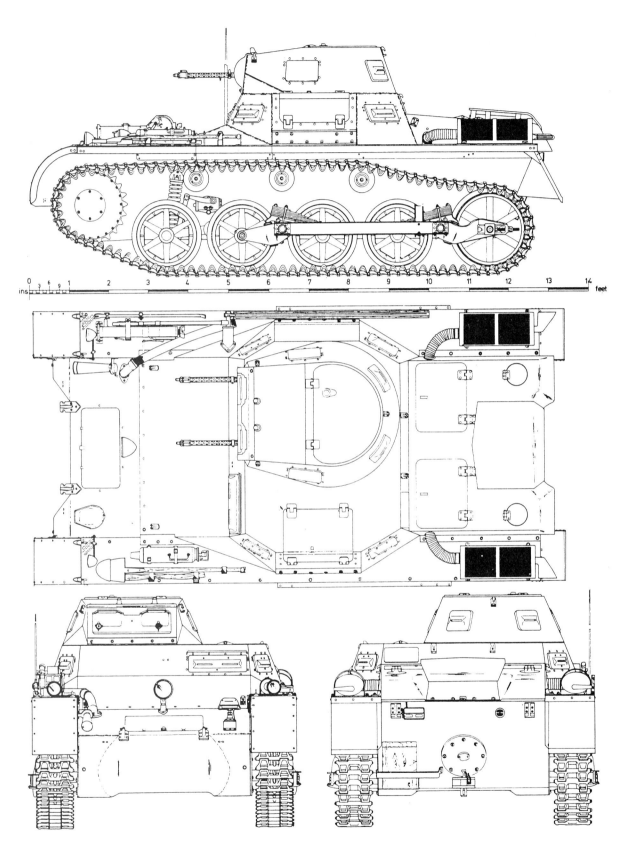

A drawing made by me of the *PzKpfw I Ausf.A* reproduced here to a scale where the bar code shows 10.5mm = 1 foot. Using a pocket calculator and the scale tables in this section work out the reduction to the scale of your choice. If you have access to a photocopier that enlarges and decreases so much the better.

A card filing system is cheap, easy to compile and maintain, and information can be found quickly. All that's needed to begin is a box and a set of index cards, which can be found on sale in most stationers. My British head-dress file 1800–1900 is shown with some of the illustrations filed therein pulled to show how they can be withdrawn for modelling purposes.

The simple notebook is hard to beat, especially if you stick to one subject per book. This cheap chain-store hardback ruled exercise book serves me well with details on British infantry shakos 1800 onwards. Over the years pictures have been collected, cut out of magazines, photographed in museums, etc., and stuck in opposite my handwritten notes.

A good SLR camera is essential to the serious modeller. You need not spend a lot and cameras in good condition can be snapped up second-hand. I use the Olympus OM system and picked up the OM1 (body only) shown here for £60 in a private sale. This camera is basic, has a mechanical shutter and can fulfil most tasks . . . recording the real thing and photographing models with the screw on +2 close-up dioptre in front of it.

The kind of invaluable reference shot the modeller should aim for. You won't always get this close (these ex-Polish army T34/85 tanks are in England!) but keep your eye open for every opportunity for reference material that will further your modelling skills and add to a reference bank of information.

graphs and ensure it is always parallel to the camera. Allowing for natural distortion depending on what type of lens is used, the measuring rod can be quite accurate when interpreting photographs for modelling purposes. This will be invaluable for the finer details. If you only have photographs to work from, you will not be able to obtain a completely accurate drawing but, with care, you should achieve a passable and workable set of elevations. Only very few drawings are the result of measuring and examining the real thing!

For working from photographs you must also have a set of dimensions or, at least an accurate overall length, and from the photographs calculate the other measurements. Transfer these to a drawing starting with a side view.

Adequate working drawings can be made in pencil on paper. Work on a drawing board if you have one, or any suitable flat surface. Basic drawing instruments – T-square, set-squares, compasses, dividers, etc. – are not overly expensive. Project the side elevation into front, rear and plan views. Initially, stick to elementary straight line work. With a wider availability of photocopying facilities, it is possible to draw your plans in a larger scale and photo-reduce them to the scale in which you model. Finally, produce templates of each part whenever possible and use these to mark out.

If you can join a local model club, do so – there is usually someone willing to help and show you how to draw plans which should, at least, get you started.

Try to attend modelling shows whenever possible . . . you can learn such a lot from just talking to experienced modellers. Here, messers Haycock and Disley of the British Model Soldier Society demonstrate figure painting on the Society's stand at the Model Engineer Exhibition.

CHAPTER 3

TOOLS AND MATERIALS

Almost every pastime or hobby requires some form of basic tool kit and military modelling is no exception. There is no reason for the tool kit to be sophisticated or costly, although it can in time grow into quite a collection as extra tools are added. The materials used by military modellers are as varied as those used by other scale modellers of, for example, aircraft, ships and railways. Although not 'everyday' materials, they are widely available both from model shops and by mail order.

Remember, before buying a basic set of modelling tools, always obtain the best you can afford. Cheap tools do not last long and can, under some circumstances, break and injure the modeller. Do not use tools for purposes for which they were not designed – especially cutting tools – a sharp cutting edge will perform better than a blunt one, which can skip off the work and cause damage elsewhere. Observe simple safety procedures and think before you act, and don't turn what should be an enjoyable hobby session into a trip to the hospital!

TOOLS

Accurate marking out, particularly for vehicle modellers, is very important so you should carefully choose pens, pencils and scribers and assess their suitability for modelling purposes. For example, ballpoint

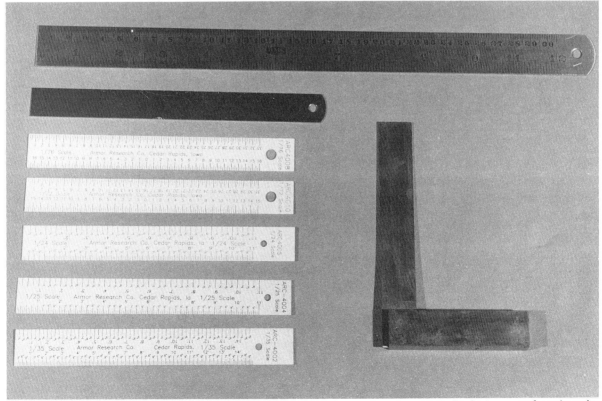

Steel rules, 12 inch and 6 inch at top along with some modellers scale rules at left. Right is a metal engineer's square so useful for checking right angles and marking out.

pens are not very useful to mark out on plastic, but certain varieties of nylon-tipped pens are.

Measuring equipment

A good quality steel rule, marked off in metric and imperial units, will perform a dual function – measuring for marking out and as a straight edge guide for cutting. Do not use a plastic rule as a straight edge guide when cutting out materials, because one slip with a sharp knife and you could ruin the rule – and your fingers! Start as you mean to continue and *never* use a plastic rule as a cutting guide. Invest in a steel rule – six inch (152mm) and one foot (305mm) types are ideal.

An asset is a steel set square for marking out perfect right angles from a known straight edge. Plastic types can be used for marking out *only* and not for cutting but, if you can equip exclusively with metal, the temptation is removed. Protractors are also handy for marking out work, as are rulers for marking parallel lines.

Vernier gauges are helpful in measuring figure heights and proportions, and the inside measurements of vehicles, or parts of them. Although they are not expensive, they have their limitations, e.g. they cannot be used as a straight cutting edge, but they do help in converting kits and determining correct proportions of anatomy for figure conversion. Callipers are useful too, but as they are expensive unless you already have them they are not really worth obtaining.

Modellers' scale rules are useful too. Armor Research Co. of Cedar Rapids, Iowa, USA, manufacture a set of rules in the popular ratios, marked off in scale feet and inches. These are a great advantage when lots of measuring has to be carried out on a project, and their use avoids the constant reference to calculator and sheets of paper for working out conversions.

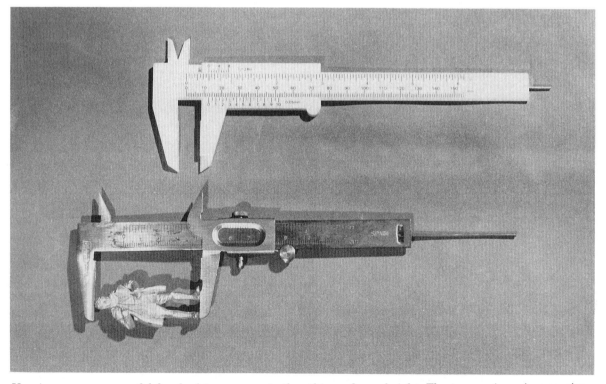

Vernier gauges are useful for checking, amongst other things, figure height. The top one is an inexpensive plastic variety, whereas the bottom one, although still not expensive, is steel.

Marking out

Pencils, especially the automatic clutch type with a fine lead, are ideal for marking out. Points 0.3mm are available for the finest lines, although a point of 0.5mm is suitable for general work. The fine tips of these pencils are designed for use with a straight edge and, unlike conventional wooden/graphite pencils, retain their points at the touch of a button. Technical pens, such as Rotring and Staedler, are useful for many tasks, though not essential.

Avoid ballpoint pens, as already mentioned, because their ink smudges on plastic and sometimes on paper too. Being greasy, the ink is not compatible with the smooth shiny surface of plastic or white metal. Besides, the rolling ball picks up surface fibres and dust and clogs. Fibre and nylon-tipped pens are more suited to modelling work and give a harder and finer line with only little pressure needed.

A set of compasses and dividers will be required for drawing and marking out circles and transferring dimensions from plan to material. A combined compass cutting tool is also an asset, and is mentioned later. An engineer's steel scriber is useful for marking out plastic card because it is possible to score and break this material (along a scribed line) quite easily.

Cutting tools

A good quality modelling knife or a scalpel is essential. There are no real substitutes, and single-edged razor blades and suchlike should not be used. Two knives, initially, are needed – one for normal light work. e.g. cutting out parts from flat sheet, cutting small parts and small carving

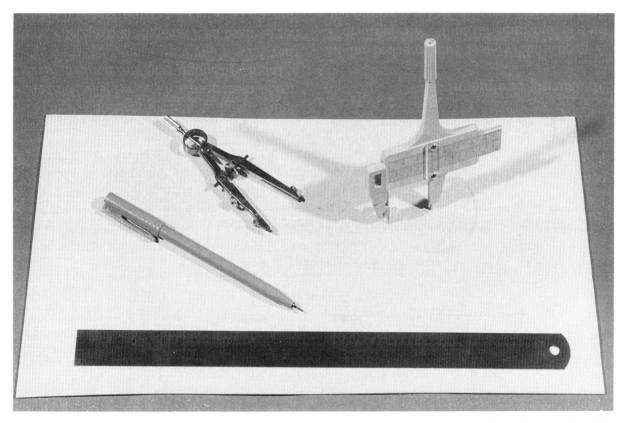

Marking out on plastic sheet must be correct and accurate. A good steel rule is essential, a nylon tipped pen is best and a small pair of compasses and compass cutter absolutely essential for cutting circles for wheels and such.

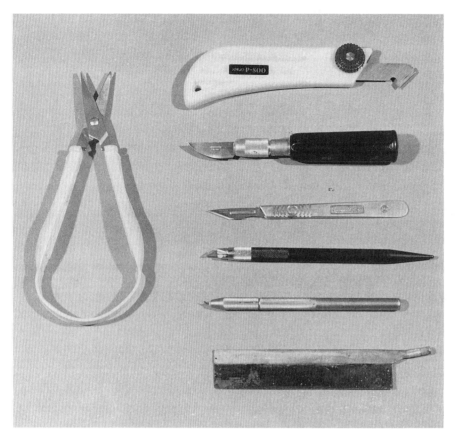

Cutting tools: always buy the best knife you can afford and use the correct weight of knife for the job in hand. *Far left* are snips – handy for rough cutting thin plastic and very thin metals. *Left, top to bottom*: Olfa line scriber; X-Acto handle with medium weight blade; Swann Morton scalpel – a good 'all rounder'; two small bladed knives for very fine work; the X-Acto razor saw blade. *Bottom*: a jewellers' adjustable piercing saw is excellent for fine work.

tasks, and one with a thicker and stouter blade for heavier work. The latter is especially helpful for heavy carving on tough materials.

Choose your knives carefully and buy ones that 'fit' your hand and are comfortable to work with. If you have a large hand, a knife with a small handle might not suit you, and vice-versa. The X-Acto range is very good and versatile with a large choice of blade types and handles.

Swann Morton scalpels are of good quality and will last a lifetime with only the blades, which are reasonably cheap, to replace for each model you make. These scalpels were designed for, and used by, surgeons and have been adopted by graphic design studios, etc., as well as

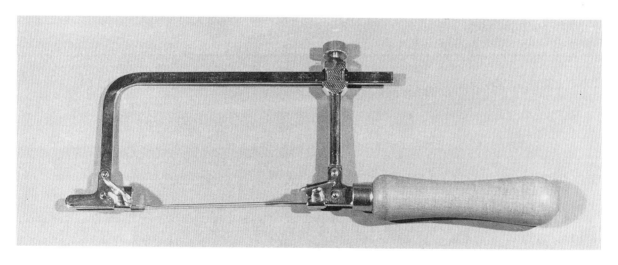

The Olfa compass cutter in action.

modellers. A number 3 handle is the most suitable for general use, and it has a large selection of blades to fit it. Model shops, local or mail order, craft material stockists or art suppliers are good sources for scalpels. Swann Morton used to make knives intended for craft work, which had brass handles and a selection of blades. The handle was later changed to plastic.

Your local DIY store will have lots of knives, often with snap-off disposable blades in magazine form contained in the handle, which are very useful for most modelling purposes. These are quite inexpensive and worth trying out.

'Razor' or slitting saws, as produced by X-Acto, are extremely useful for cutting both plastics and wood, but they are not really suited to harder materials such as metals. Although razor saws will cut white metal alloy effectively, any thick pieces will cause the saw to bind and the teeth to clog. A coping or piercing saw is a much better tool for cutting and converting white metal figures. 'Junior' hacksaws have their place and can be used to remove large pieces of white metal in conversion work. Slitting discs can be used in miniature motor tools and these are covered in the appropriate section.

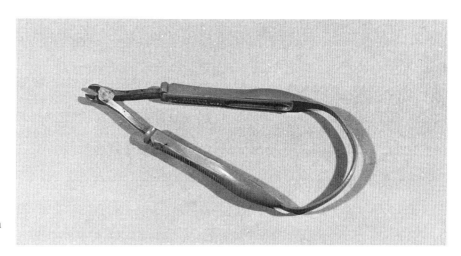

Fine nippers used to remove plastic parts from their moulding sprues.

A compass cutter, mentioned in the section on marking out equipment, (page 19), is a helpful tool. Perhaps the best known variant is that made by Olfa of Japan. Working in a similar manner to conventional compasses, an angled cutting blade is fitted instead of a lead. The cutting blades are also available for compasses found in drawing sets.

By continuous scribing, perfect circles can be cut from card or plastic card and this is useful for making up, for example, wheels from laminated sections of plastic card. A lathe with which to turn up wheels is not usually found in the average military modeller's collection of tools.

Snips or nippers are very handy for plastic kit modellers, as they enable kit parts to be cleanly removed from the sprues. Where white metal parts are cast on sprues, nippers are the best method of removing the parts without destroying any detail. They are handier than a knife and safer than twisting parts away from the

A graver being used on a master pattern by a figure designer. This is Sid Horton of Chota Sahib.

sprue, which can lead to damage of the part. They will also cut thin wire, either the soft fuse wires used by modellers or the harder rigid brass and steel wires and small diameter rods. Ordinary household scissors have their place, though they should never be used for accurate cutting – always leave this to the knife. However, they are useful for rough cutting out of card and thin plastic sheet.

Gouges and gravers are cutting tools used for sculpting figures. Small blades in handles are produced for the miniaturist and these can be obtained from art and craft shops.

Abrasives

Sanding down and cleaning off to an acceptable smooth finish is a task that takes time and practice, with both metal files and abrasive papers.

The military modeller needs files and plenty of them. There are three basic types of small files – needle, riffler and warding files. The cutting edges, the toothed pattern, of files clog easily when filing soft white metal, so avoid this by putting talcum powder on the teeth before you begin. Plastic can be removed with a wire brush, which can also remove large white metal deposits, though once white metal clogs in a file it's very difficult to remove, and can only be done effectively with thin shim run through each tooth cut to remove the metal deposits.

Files come in six basic different shapes: round, square, three-square, flat, hand and half-round. Needle files do not usually have handles and are about 5½in (140mm) long, whereas warding files have wooden

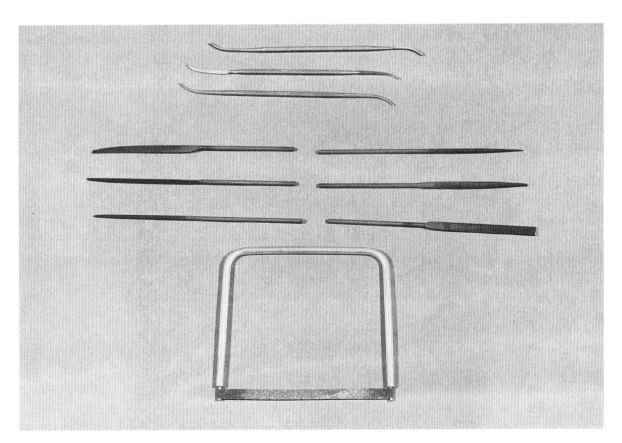

Files! Top are three rifflers, centre six different needle files and bottom is a 'flexi-file'. The latter is a frame that holds strips of emery cloth.

Sanding down a resin
tank turret on a flat sheet
of emery paper.

handles, are larger overall and are about 7in (178mm) long. Small riffler files are versatile, about 6in long, and are double-ended with curved, pointed and shaped ends, enabling filing of hard-to-reach places. Although they are expensive, they tend to be better than straight-bladed needle files due to their curved blades. Made of chrome vanadium, files will last a long time if cared for and reserved for only light work such as modelling. Do not use them for heavy domestic tasks for which they are not designed. A rat or mouse tail flexible file is a round-section file and is useful for enlarging holes and suchlike. It can be made to bend slightly and some round-section files are manufactured as 'flexi-files' for just this purpose. In time they will break after continuous bending.

Abrasives such as 'sandpaper' (which is an incorrect colloquial term used freely as a generic group name), emery and wet-and-dry, together with Scotchbrite (a trade name), are all the modeller needs for general work. Wire wool is handy on white metal figures, as is a fibreglass brush. However, the latter is made up of small

fibres which can shed tiny sharp 'bristles' which can get into the skin and cause irritation which can be painful.

'Sandpaper' is really glasspaper, but in everyday language has lent its incorrect generic name to an easily recognisable group of descriptive terms – 'sanding down', 'sanding disc', etc. It is intended for wood, whereas emery paper (made from corundum powder) is stronger and is for use on metal. Wet-and-dry papers are made from silicon carbide and are intended to be used with water which acts as a lubricant when sanding (there's that term again!) surfaces and helps to stop the grit clogging. As the name suggests, these can be dry too.

'Scotchbrite', produced by 3M, is a type of plastic 'wire wool' and is excellent for smoothing and polishing plastic. It can also be used on white metal and is reason-ably priced.

A fairly recent innovation for the motor tool is a range of abrasive rubber discs or wheels which have silicon bound in them, and these are ideal for polishing white metal. They come in various sizes and grades and remove minute amounts of white metal, and so are suitable on small parts. Wear a dust mask when using these discs; they create a lot of particles which are easily breathed in through the nose and mouth. Try blowing your nose after a session with one and no mask and you will see what I mean!

Drills

The word 'drill' to the layman, if applied to modelling in miniature, conjures up visions of mini-motorised drills (see under Power Tools) with micro-twist drill bits. While there is a place for motorised drills, many experienced modellers, especially those working with plastics, would rather use a small hand drill or pin vice – also known as a pin chuck, which is a more accurate description. A pin vice is also a small hand vice! Unless a speed control is fitted, motorised tools tend to melt plastic rather than drill it cleanly.

White metal can be difficult to drill for precisely the same reason – friction causes heat and the drill binds. Really it's a matter of experimenting on various materials.

The pin chuck, which is usually supplied with different sized collets, is rotated between the fingers and it ensures control especially on very small parts, 1/16th inch and below, such as drilling out a plastic rod section to represent a gun barrel.

Twist drills are available in all sizes from those thinner than a household pin up to the standard DIY sizes and above. To kit yourself out with everything would, of course, at first be totally impractical financially! Furthermore, small drills are not widely available and tend to be stocked by specialist suppliers.

The 'standard' range of high-speed twist drills runs from 1/16th inch to about 1/4 inch

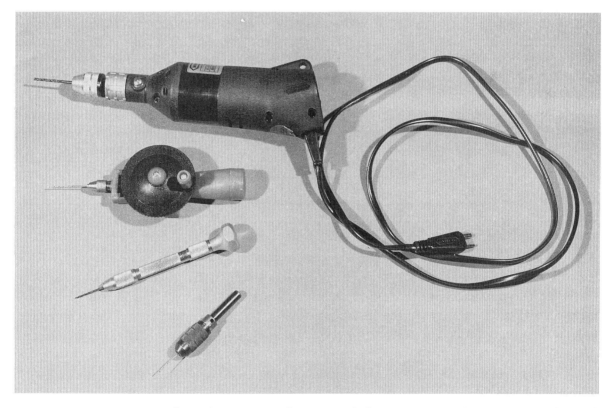

Drills! Top to bottom: Minicraft 12volt; miniature plastic hand-drill; X-Acto pin chuck (or pin vice) and a small engineer's pin chuck.

Scotchbrite abrasive pads. Those in the foreground are sold as track cleaning pads for railway modellers, whilst the larger pad behind them is marketed as a pan cleaner for the kitchen. This plastic-type abrasive material works very well on plastic, wood, resin and white metal and is an alternative to wire wool. Keep some worn pieces for fine work and finishing off.

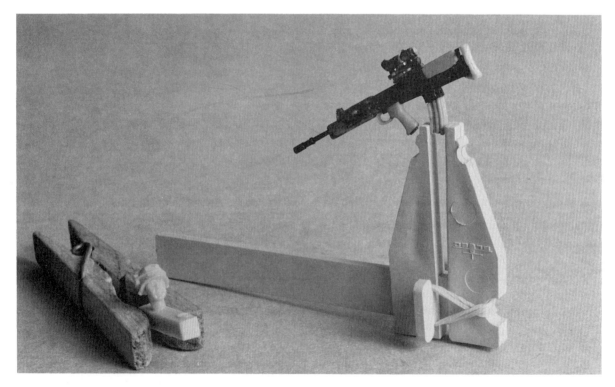

Wooden spring clothes' pegs make excellent clamps for holding smaller parts for painting and suchlike. The clamp at right, originally designed for aeromodellers, is made from plastic and employs nothing more complicated than an elastic band to make it work.

or, metric, around 1.5mm or 2mm upwards to 8mm. Quality depends on the price you pay, but generally the smaller the drill, the higher the price. Also, the mortality rate of small drills can be high in inexperienced hands and anything below a 1mm twist drill should be used very cautiously in a mini-power tool. If metal is worked on continuously, twist drills soon become blunt. It is possible to re-sharpen drills with equipment designed specially for the job.

Protect your eyes when drilling, especially if you use mini-power tools, because small drills can turn into small unguided missiles if they break during drilling. Plastic protective goggles are cheap and, although you may never have an accident, always put safety first.

For making holes in thin plastic card, a drill is not always necessary; for certain tasks, a modeller's punch and die set is ideal. These consist of blocks of metal or Perspex with accurately drilled holes of varying diameters and the corresponding hardened steel punches. Plastic card is sandwiched between the blocks which are lined up by pins at the corners, and a

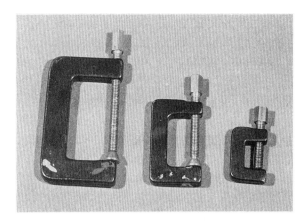

Three miniature inexpensive 'G' clamps by Draper Tools, bought in a DIY store.

punch inserted into the appropriate hole, tapped lightly with a small hammer (sometimes the punch can be pushed with the fingers on thin card) to create a clean hole. The punchings are useful for rivets, and should be stored for future use rather than discarded. Die and punch sets are not cheap. They are precision made, but will last for many years; Historex Agents of Dover, UK, can supply them (see Appendix 1 for address).

Supporting the work

It is very important to grip the material on which you are working as securely as possible. Even when painting a single white metal figure, it must be firmly supported, leaving all-round access for your paintbrush or whatever.

The conventional vice is very handy and there are specialist modellers' vices now available. One of the most useful is a plastic suction vice which clamps to a clean, smooth working surface by creating a vacuum in a nylon sucker on its under-surface. This is done by swinging a lever down to lock it. It is eminently suited to light modelling work. Small metal vices that clamp onto the workbench, a board or the kitchen table are reasonably priced and very useful.

A miniature plastic suction vice. The lever on the side controls the sucker mounted on the base enabling the device to be attached to a smooth surface.

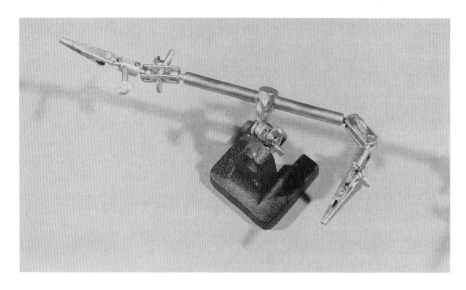

'Helping Hands' are extremely useful. They range in price and examples can be found for a few pounds.

A home-made clamp can be made by fixing spring clothes' pegs to a wooden block which, along with rubber bands, can hold small painted parts to dry.

Pliers, especially the varieties made for smaller work and modelling, should be added to your tool kit as soon as possible. Snipe and round nose types, including a pair with side cutters, are all you need to begin with. Wire is difficult to bend, especially if it's the harder type, and pliers are just the ticket to handle it.

All clamps, from the small pin vice to larger engineering types, are useful, though the pin vice is the best to buy first. Plastic modelmakers' clamps, which are

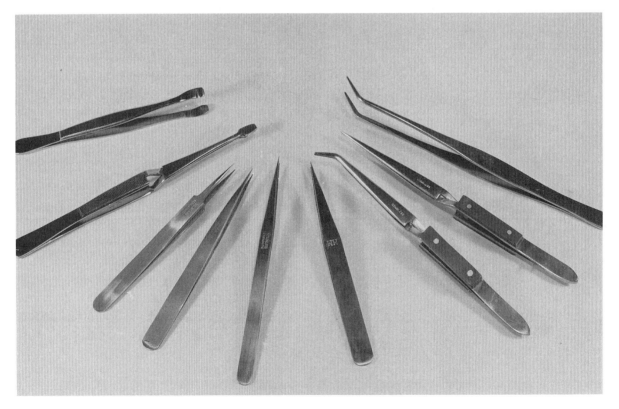

A variety of tweezers ranging from fine needle points to spoon ends. The tweezers second and third from right are opposite action and hold parts without pressure being maintained.

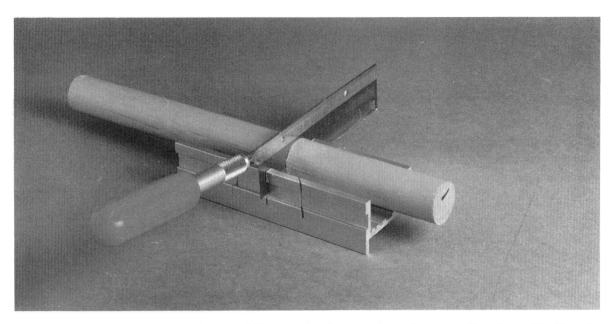

A simple clamp for holding 54mm figures while you paint them can be made very easily at home. You'll need a piece of wooden dowel, thick plastic card or thin wood, two small nuts and bolts, two cabinet makers' turn buttons (DIY shops sell them) and a wood screw.

Saw off a piece of wooden dowel to suit the size of your hand; aim for the length that suits you best. If the handle is too long you can catch it on the table when you are painting. The dowel is being sawed in an aluminium mitre box here to keep things all 'square' initially.

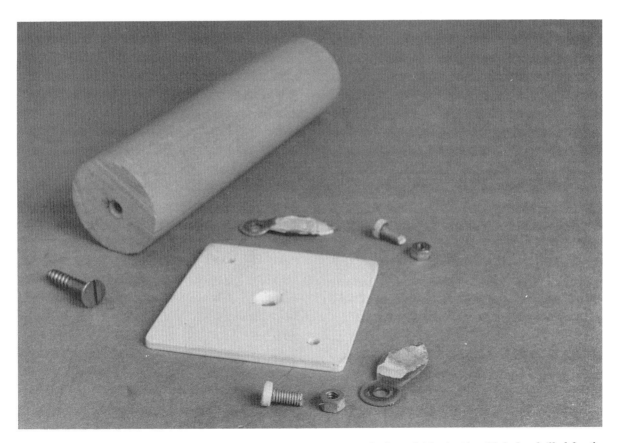

The components; dowel drilled to take the wood screw, a table made from thick plastic with holes drilled for the turn buttons at two corners and the wood screw through the centre.

The unit assembled. Obviously home-made, but simple and efficient in operation. You do not need to touch the figure again once it's clamped in place thus protecting what you've painted from the natural oils in your finger tips which can ruin a painted surface.

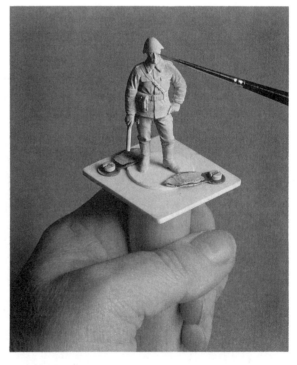

A 1:35 scale Hornet figure clamped into place ready for painting. The figure has been temporarily glued to a circular base cut from plastic sheet.

Painting about to commence. The unit is comfortable to hold – there's no rough edges and it can be braced against the workbench or whatever to keep everything steady for painting those little details . . . such as the eyes!

held together by nothing more complicated than an elastic band, are cheap and effective.

Metal screw 'G' clamps ('C' cramps in the USA) are good for holding heavier materials, especially where soldering is being done, and they can double as 'heat sinks' in some cases, keeping heat away from previously soldered joints.

'Helping Hands' is a most useful piece of equipment available to the modeller. This consists of a heavy, cast metal base with a central adjustable base mounted on a ball and socket joint with, in turn, ball and socket joints with crocodile clips on both ends. This assembly will grip really fine work while you carry out the necessary operations on it. Shop around for 'Helping Hands' . . . they do vary in price yet basically perform the same operation.

Tweezers are the modeller's friend, and the military modeller needs more than one pair. Avoid the cheap, pressed metal types sold as part of a tool kit and buy a good pair or, better still, buy two or more pairs –

you won't regret it. Fine points with straight and angled tips are most helpful with small parts. The tweezers must be comfortable to hold and well constructed with accurate points, about five to six inches long. Keep the tips clean and do not allow paint or adhesives to collect on them. Opposite action tweezers are worth considering, too. These grip the object in the points without pressure being maintained on the shafts. When pressure is applied, the points open – quite the reverse to the conventional tweezers.

A very useful aid for holding a figure for painting is very easy to make at home and is shown in the photograph on this page. Figures, plastic or white metal, up to 65mm, can be held securely and all that is needed is a handle, a flat 'table' of wood, though plastic or Perspex is more suitable, about 1½in × 1½in (38mm × 38mm), two small bolts with wing nuts and two metal strips. You can use brass turnbuttons of the types used in music and cigarette box making.

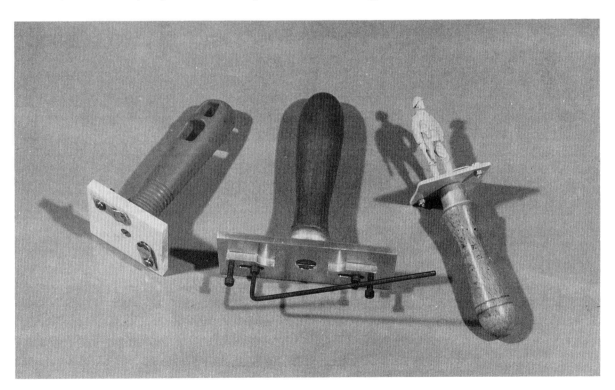

Three figure clamps. The one far left and centre are commercial products, whereas the other is home-made using a file handle, thick plastic card and cabinet makers' turn buttons.

The 'table' is fixed to the handle, a wooden or plastic file handle makes a good one, and the strips positioned at opposite corners. The figure's base is held by the strips and the illustration explains it all. I would advise making more than one and try varying the dimensions to enable larger figures to be accommodated. After all, most modellers have more than one figure under construction or being painted at any one time. When a painting session ends, the handle can be placed in an empty jam jar leaving the work upright ready for next time.

Motor tools

Motor tools, either battery or transformer, are a tremendous boon to the military modeller. Not only do they accept drills, but also slitting discs, saws, burrs, and many other attachments. Avoid cheap motor tools and go for a good branded name. Cheap motor tools vibrate and are not easy to control even with speed controllers, and the motors can burn out much quicker than a better model. Vertical drill presses and stands are available to hold the drill and can be added as your power tool kit grows. If possible, try the tools before you buy.

A wire cup and circular type brush fitted to a power tool is a time-saving device for cleaning up white metal figures, and it gets into all the inaccessible places. However, do not overdo any wire brush work as, although it is a labour-saver, it can also destroy some of the fine engraving on the model.

Later, with practice, engraving tips and burrs in the mini drill will enable you to experience a whole new approach on detailing white metal figures. Visit a stockist and see just what is on offer; it's amazing just how many attachments and

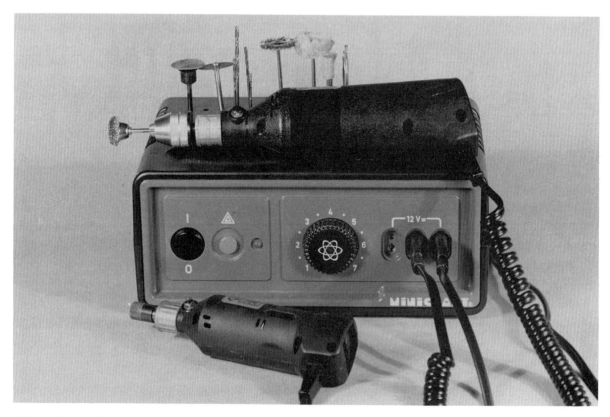

Minicraft variable speed controller and accessories power point. Two drills are fitted here and there is a selection of tools on top of the unit.

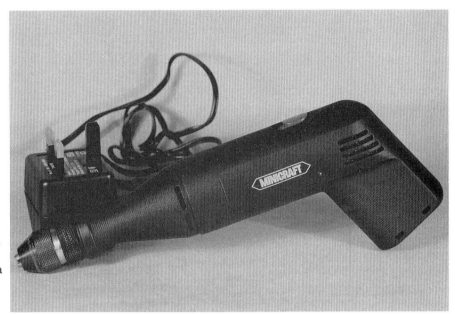

Right: Minicraft re-
chargeable drill. *Below*: a
Minicraft drill fitted with
a brass wire cup brush – a
labour saving way of
cleaning up white metal
castings.

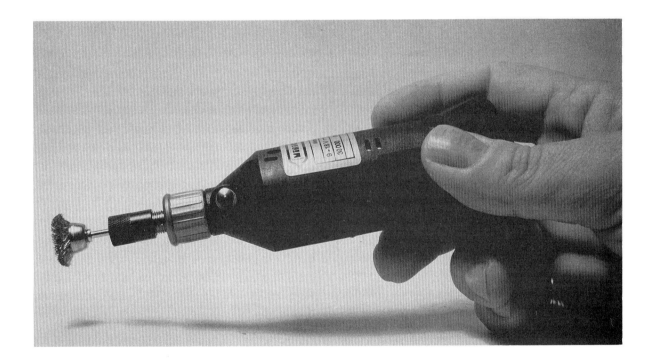

different types of miniature motorised tools there are available to the modeller nowadays.

Soldering irons

As with most specialist tools, soldering irons benefit from a lot of practice. Novices rarely achieve perfect soldered joints initially and many do not progress past the first steps, deciding it's too much bother and resorting to some of the modern types of glues rather than persevering with hot iron, flux and solder.

Soldering is simply the joining of two metal surfaces with the application of heat

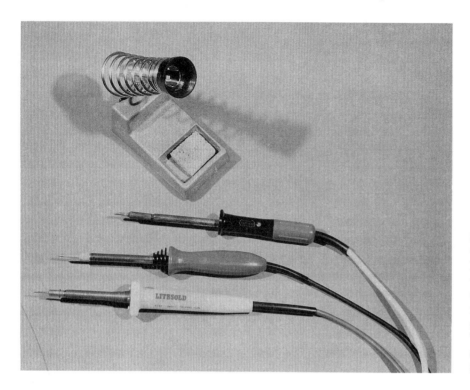

Soldering irons for use on white metal with a holder/heat sink fitted with a foam pad to wipe the iron's tip. All are mains irons (240volts) and are, top to bottom; Varistat 50watt; Oryx 50watt; Litesold 50watt (electronic control).

and liquid metal (the solder) whose flow is controlled in and along the joint with flux.

Soldering is not difficult if you remember some very basic rules. All joints to be soldered must be scrupulously cleaned, the correct flux selected, an iron capable of delivering the required heat for the metal being joined, and, if possible, both the iron and solder should be brought to the joint simultaneously.

Military modellers, especially white metal figure kit assemblers, will find that a soldered joint is superior to one made with glue. In addition, the very nature of low-melt solder enables it to act as a filler, so dispensing with the need for fillers on joints which are less than perfect. AFV modellers also may need to replace fine plastic, or overscale and incorrect items, with wire or metal rod, and such assemblies benefit from soldered construction.

For white metal, a special low-melt solder is needed, plus the appropriate flux and, of course, a low-temperature soldering iron, because most white metal alloys used in model figure casting melt around and over 95°C (200°F). Therefore, the solder must have a lower melting point and most commercially available low-melt solders liquefy around 70°C. Properties of these solders, and they are simply lower melting point alloys, vary, but those for modelling will have gap-filling capabilities which is to the modeller's advantage.

Flux used for white metal is a clear organic type, active at low temperatures, but it is corrosive if left on the soldered joints. It must always be washed away with warm water. Finally, I often immerse the soldered model in warm water with washing-up liquid added which cleans away all of the flux, especially in difficult-to-reach places. A scrub down with an old toothbrush helps, too. This holds true for almost all fluxes and it is good practice whenever possible to flush all joints immediately after soldering.

Avoid inhaling any vapours given off from soldered joints, as they are not only unpleasant but could be harmful. If you're working close-in on a job, wear a mask to avoid solder fumes.

Soldering irons with some sort of heat control are the most suitable, and those operating with a bi-metal control strip are ideal. A standard iron can be modified with some form of voltage control (such as a dimmer switch) wired into its power supply, but this should be left to someone qualified or experienced in electrics. However, commercially available devices for temperature control are available.

A suitable iron for white metal work is a conversion to a photographic tacking iron, as assembled by Litesold for Carr's Modelling Products. Rated at 50 watts, the regulated tip temperature is 70°C, maintained 100 times a second via solid state circuitry in the handle. The makers claim accuracy to within less than one degree. This iron is eminently suited to fine work and smaller joins.

Alec Tiranti also market an iron, an Oryx Model 50, rated at 50 watts. Similar in operation to the Carr's iron, this one will tackle most jobs and comes with two different tips, the solder and flux. It makes a very good starting kit for the modeller.

When soldering many joints in a close area, it will be found that, due to heat transmission through metal, the iron's application can cause previously soldered joints to become unsoldered! This can happen, for example, on wire used for a

vehicle tilt frame of the type used to support a canvas sheet over the rear open body of a military truck. A heat sink is the answer. This is basically a piece or pieces of metal secured around a joint to block or divert the heat from already soldered joints in the vicinity. A crocodile clip, of the type used in electric circuitry, is the most convenient method to use, because of its easy application and removal and its good heat conduction. For a larger sink, crocodile clips can be used to clamp a sheet of metal in place.

When using irons other than low temperature types, it is advisable to employ some form of heat sink for the tip while it is in use over long periods. Conducting heat away from the soldering iron's tip or bit will prolong the tip's life and enable its easy removal, and will prevent it from becoming 'heat sealed' into the iron and thereby rendering it useless as a unit. A large block of metal for the tip to rest on is ideal, and any heavy cast iron base would suffice as long as heat is able to flow from the tip to be dispersed through the 'sink'. Alternatively, buy a stand specifically made for the purpose.

Always use the correct soldering iron for the job. It's pointless trying a small iron designed for repairing printed circuits on a large mass such as white metal – even if

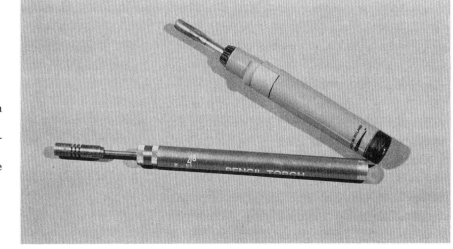

Mini pencil torches run on butane gas. They can be used on white metal (carefully!) where sufficient mass is present; otherwise they come into their own using solder paste on supported and jigged assemblies of brass and steel etched parts.

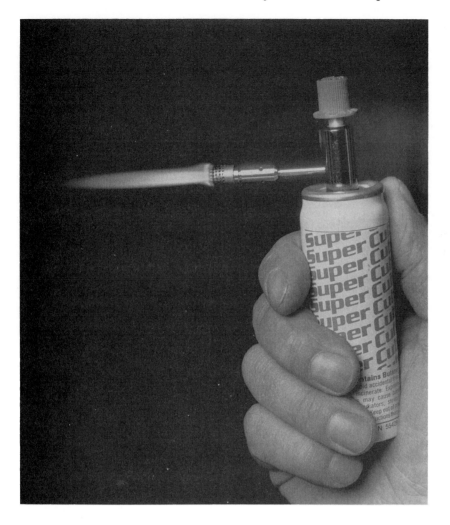

The Super Cub mini blow-torch is fine for precision work. The hand gives a good indication of the size of the unit.

the tip temperatures are low. It just won't work!

For some time I have been using a mini blow torch, or 'pencil torch', which runs on butane gas, for assembling larger white metal kits where bulk has defeated the use of heating up the joints with the conventional soldering iron. It is especially good for assembling large-scale cast white metal horse kits. I tin each joining surface with the iron, clamp the job with soft wire and then run the torch along the joins to melt the solder and seal them. It takes practice: too close and you'll turn the white metal into liquid! The distance of the torch flame from the job is critical – the idea is to melt the solder, not the white metal. I developed the process from practising on

pieces of white metal from kits until I got it right.

The pyrogravure

The pyrogravure is a very useful tool for modellers who do most, if not all, of their work in plastic. The pen-shaped pyrogravure has a needle tip and operates on a 4.5 volt supply, so it's safe and will not burn the fingers badly if the tip is accidentally touched.

Working from a combined mains plug transformer, the pyrogravure is easy to use and the modeller will soon become proficient in its use. It melts most plastics, but is best on the polystyrene types; ABS plastics can be worked, but not as easily.

For texturing – melting the surface of plastic – many techniques are possible; e.g. hair on figures and horses will certainly benefit from the pyrogravure's use, as will battle damage on plastic vehicle models. The anti-magnetic paste, zimmerit, applied to German tanks during WWII, can be cut into plastic surfaces with a pyrogravure, giving a most realistic finish in most scales except the very large.

The single-heat type is all the modeller should need under normal circumstances, although for heavier work vari-heat models are available. Designed for wood and leather burning, or 'poker work', these pyrogravures are supplied with different tips to enable a variety of cuts and marks to be made. Although a little on the large side for 'small-scale modellers', they can be most useful for work on model buildings, large-scale vehicles and scenic model terrain. Such pyrography sets are more expensive than the single heat type.

Magnifying glasses

Under normal conditions, a magnifying glass is not needed for modelling purposes, but wearers of spectacles and those whose eyes are 'not as good as they used to be' may need some form of assistance.

Stand magnifiers will aid painting of small-scale figurines, though 'working under the glass' does take some getting used to. It is not as easy to work under a glass as it is with the naked eye. Consider the length of the paintbrush handle – invariably it fouls the magnifying lens if this is not mounted at an appropriate

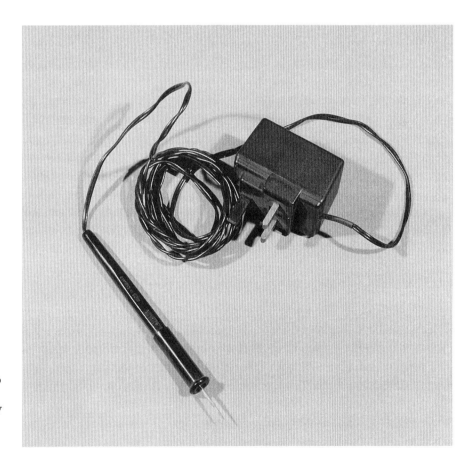

A 4.5volt pyrogravure as marketed by Historex Agents of Dover. The mains plug contains a step-down transformer supplying only 4.5volts to the copper working tip which heats it sufficiently to work polystyrene plastics.

distance, or the work, in relation to the lens, is badly placed, a fault of co-ordination which must be mastered before a comfortable relationship with a stand magnifier can be made.

Small magnifying lenses, with suction pads for attaching to spectacles, or clip-on types, will be the answer to many modellers' needs. Such optical devices are not cheap but, if you need some form of clip-on magnifying lens, seek advice from a registered optician, particularly if you intend attaching it to spectacles. Magnifying spectacles are also available, but again consult an optician first.

Jewellers', watchmakers' or toolmakers' loupes (eye-cup type magnifiers) are not really suitable for the modeller, especially for long period usage. Although they are reasonable in price, gripping such a device in one eye for long periods will not only become tedious but impossible.

Illuminated magnifiers are expensive, although a lot of figure modellers use them for close work such as painting faces on small-scale figures or for painting flat figures. If you become used to working with glass, fine – but if you don't need one to begin with, even better.

MATERIALS

The materials used by military modellers fall into four basic groups: plastics, metals, woods and paper or card.

Plastics

There are thousands of different plastics in general modelling use. They all have similar properties and fall into two groups – *thermoplastics* which can be melted down, thus retaining plastic characteristics, and *thermoset* which, once set, cannot be reduced to their original state.

Polystyrene Plastics of the polystyrene type are the most commonly encountered. 'Plastic kits' are moulded in polystyrene as are figures, 'plastic card' sheets used for scratchbuilding and parts for conversions.

Polystyrene is brittle and, in order to ensure a small amount of elasticity, rubber polymers are introduced. In this form, polystyrene is known as 'high impact'. Its working temperature when it becomes fluid for injection moulding is around 75°C.

Plastic card is the general everyday term for sheets of polystyrene, extruded into varying thicknesses, usually .010 – .060 inch, in .010 divisions. This can be scored, i.e. cut half through then snapped along the line to produce a clean cut. It can be drilled, carved and moulded by heat forming or vacuum formed with appropriate equipment.

Polystyrene sheet comes in various colours and is also embossed in useful patterns such as brick and stone work, planking, corrugated, etc. Polystyrene rod and tube are also commercially available. Polystyrene can be moulded as clear sheet, but it must be in its original brittle state (i.e. no rubber added and therefore not high impact) for clarity. Expanded polystyrene foam is produced by gas expansion into a lower density cellular form.

Polystyrene can be glued with liquid or polystyrene 'cements', which consist of polystyrene dissolved in solvents such as ethylene dichloride or carbon tetrachloride.

ABS (Acrylobutyl Styrene) ABS is similar to polystyrene in appearance but it is a more expensive medium of high impact strength. It can be treated in the same way as polystyrene and produces excellent injection mouldings of thinner gauge. It is also available in sheet form and as clear sheet, and lots of different shapes and mouldings are produced by 'Plastruct', a company specialising in ABS production

Painting a flat figurine, step-by-step. This example is a 30mm scale mounted Roman officer by Droste of Germany.

1. After cleaning the casting of any flash it is undercoated with matt white enamel or acrylic to provided a 'tooth' for the oil paint used.

2. Flesh areas are shown blocked in and shaded. A mixture of Talens Yellow Ochre, Flesh Ochre and Titanium White oil paints were used for the flesh colour.

3. The leather body armour, helmet and crest and cloak are blocked in, shaded and highlighted. Do not use black for shading colours, or white to highlight, but complementary colours, blending in well whilst the paint is wet and easy to work. Any mistakes can be cleaned off and the process begun again.

4. Saddle cloth and the rider's boot painted. A decision as to the horse's final colour should be made now.

5. A cream horse is not easy to paint. Shading and high-lights have to be subdued or the effect will be ruined by colours with too much contrast. Don't forget the correct hoof colours too!

6. The final touches. Harnessing and reins with their metal ornaments finish the job. Do not use metallic paint for these, try depicting the metal with shading and highlighting techniques on the basic colour. Initially, it's wise to practise off the figure, to get it right.

Any shadows should now be added, such as those cast on the horse's neck by the reins.

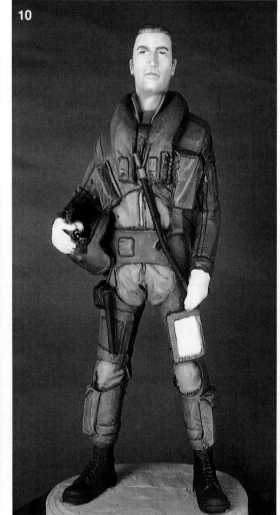

Painting a face with artists' oil colours is not difficult once you've grasped the basic fundamentals. Try this easy step-by-step approach first and then perfect it with your own technique. The figure is a 1:7 scale modern day Royal Air Force pilot in pressure suit by Ballantynes of Walkerburn.

1. White undercoat – matt enamel or acrylic will do fine.

2. Flesh undercoat blocked in. Talens Flesh Ochre, Yellow Ochre and Titanium White were the three colours used for the basic flesh tone.

3. Darker flesh tone in shaded areas, such as eye sockets, sides of nose, under lips.

4. Lighter flesh tones blended in by adding more white and Yellow Ochre to the mixture . . . but don't overdo this.

5. Hair and eyebrows painted on mixed from Ultramarine Blue and Burnt Sienna for a dark brown colour.

6. Paint eyeballs white with a slight touch of blue.

7. Eyeballs painted in, the centres of which must correspond with the corners of the mouth when looking directly ahead. The eye is brown with a black pupil.

8. The upper and lower lids painted and defined over the eyeball. Look at your own eyes in a mirror for guidance.

9. The eyes are finished and when dry benefit from a thin coat of acrylic varnish, which doesn't yellow. The hair is highlighted with Yellow Ochre.

10. Painting the face is now complete. A start can be now made on the flight clothing. Note: This step-by-step sequence, it must be emphasized, is a very basic approach and is easily improved upon once perfected.

1

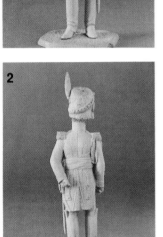

2

3

4

5

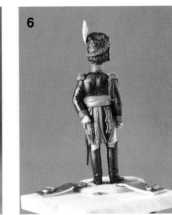

6

7

8

9

10

Painting a 54mm scale miniature figurine using a basic system with artists' oil colours. The model is a personality figurine of Major General Dorsenne 1st Foot Grenadiers (1773–1812), French army c. 1812, by Le Cimier of Paris.

1. Castings assembled and undercoated with matt white acrylic.

2. Rear view of the assembled and undercoated figurine.

3. Clamped on a handle the figure's face is painted in the same basic sequence as shown in the face painting section.

4. Dark blue and black areas blocked in with thinned black enamel or acrylic paint as a key for the oil paint.

5. Cuffs, collar and rest of uniform receives the initial thin covering of oil colours, brushed out to eliminate any ridges or build up of paint.

6. Rear of figure showing painted work so far in the sequence.

7. All highlighted areas receive attention.

8. Metallic colours added on bearskin cap plate, sword hilt, buttons, etc. Metallic shoulder lace is Yellow Ochre highlighted with added Naples Yellow and white with a little gold acrylic added for sparkle when dry.

9. All finished! Only the base needs to be painted or dressed with scenic materials.

10. Rear view of the completed job . . . don't forget the spurs!

1

6

2

7

3

8

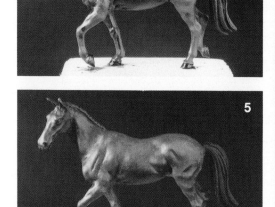

4

5

9

Oil paints are an ideal choice of medium for painting horses, being more easily blended because of their slow drying time and slight sheen. Remember, in general, only greys appear matt.

1. The assembled kit fixed to a block of wood via wires let into holes drilled in the horse's hoofs and undercoated with thinned, matt white acrylic. Don't guess, use a colour book for guidance when painting horses. The colour chosen here was a Bright Bay.

2. First coat of dark brown paint is applied over the undercoat.

3. First coat applied, brushed out and the darker mane and tail blocked in.

4. Shaded areas painted in.

5. Shaded areas blended in.

6. Highlighted areas laid on.

7. Highlighted areas blended in.

8. Facial markings, socks and muzzle painted.

9. Finished! Note the slight dappling on the rump.

Some of Graham Dixey's painted flats are shown on this page. Graham was instrumental in furthering the popularity of the flat figure in the United Kingdom and was a founder member of the British Flat Figure Society.

Top, a Chinese chariot, c.800BC.

Left, 'A visit to the hat shop'. These are 30mm figures of the Napoleonic period.

Bottom left, a larger 54mm flat – 'A Knight of Nurnberg'.

A Knight of Nürnberg

Above, Toronaga and Blackthorne; 30mm flats from the Shogun series by Oldhafer. (*Photographs: Graham Dixey*.)

A tribute to the late Bill
Hearne is this, his last
90mm figurine kit of a
British 11th Hussar as he
would have appeared in the
Crimea, perhaps during the
famous Charge of the Light
Brigade. The horse is shown
during the painting
sequence and the assembled
kit finished totally in acrylic
colours. Bill's tragic death in
1991 left quite a gap in the
ranks of figure designers
working in the United
Kingdom. Unfortunately,
the production of his models
after his death did not
continue.

Mounted figures are popular among figure modellers. *Top* is a 90mm study of Napoleon riding his famous grey, Marengo, designed by David Cope of Invicta. This figure is painted in acrylics. *Bottom left*, a US cavalryman by Andrea Miniatures of Spain in 54mm scale. Horse and rider are painted in oil colours. *Bottom right*, Lawrence of Arabia, also by Andrea and to 54mm scale, was painted in enamels and acrylic colours.

Top, back and front views of Poste Militaire's Officer of von Ratsky's Hussars, painted in oil colours. This figure is a superb sculpture in 75mm scale for Poste Militaire by the talented American designer, Mike Good. Reference to photos of Leopards is necessary to obtain the correct pattern for the spots on the skin worn by this hussar. *Bottom*, a 90mm scale 95th Rifleman from the Peninsular War period. This was the last figure completed by the late Richard Almond, a young and very talented designer. The unpainted casting is also shown with its split base design to accept the accompanying figure which was nearly completed when Richard died. Fortunately the work of Richard Almond lives on marketed by his widow Jackie under the Almond Miniatures banner. The second rifleman kit was finished and is available at the time of writing.

for model makers. ABS can, like polystyrene, be joined with a solution of ABS and a solvent such as ethyl isobutyl ketone. ABS can be stuck to polystyrene with this solvent, though polystyrene glues are not successful in joining ABS plastics. ABS melts at around the same temperatures as polystyrene.

Acrylic ('Perspex') 'Perspex' is the trade name ('Plexiglass in the USA) for acrylic plastics and, although expensive, clear acrylic can be used by modellers for display cases and scenic modellers for representing water where its surface can be worked with a solvent or heat to produce ripples, etc. Acrylic can be moulded and needs its own cement or solvent to stick it. The thinner acrylic is, the more brittle it becomes.

Polythene Polythene (or more correctly *polyethylene*) is used for moulding figures, normally found in the popular scales 1:32, 1:76 and 1:72. It is a soft plastic with a 'greasy' surface and is practically impossible to paint or glue together. In fact, the action of oil-based enamel paints on polythene figures tends to produce a surface hardening which makes the material become brittle in the long term. Although resistant to solvents sticking it, it 'soaks in' oils used in paints! It can be sealed – in the case of figurines, by coating with watered-down PVA glues which will accept all known model paints without gradual deterioration.

It is virtually impossible to glue polystyrene, and any successful conversion work on figures must be made with a very sharp knife blade and joints reinforced with pins or similar before the completed conversion is coated with diluted PVA glue as a primer.

Polythene has a lower melting point than polystyrene at around 50°C – 60°C depending on its density.

Expanded polystyrene Perhaps best known for its use as a packaging material for everyday products, expanded polystyrene can be adapted by the modeller mainly for scenic work. Being very light, it is useful for making hills and ground work and, to a limited extent, buildings.

Consisting of gas-expanded polystyrene cells, the material is not easy to cut, although a very fine 'saw-type' blade will produce a clean cut if used carefully. For finished work, a hot wire cutter is best. These are powered by a battery and operate on about 4.5–6 volts and can easily be made from a frame of wood plastic or metal with a wire stretched between. Of course, if the frame is metal the wire needs to be insulated from it. Use the thinnest wire possible for the cutter. Sticking expanded polystyrene must be done with water-based adhesives, because most other solvents simply melt it. The same goes for paints! Use only water-based types on expanded polystyrene.

Resins

Resins are thermoset plastics. By mixing two agents, they eventually produce, by chemical action, a rigid plastic substance which, before setting, can be poured into a mould or former to produce copies of a master model. Two basic types will be found in use – polyester and polyurethane.

Polyester resins are brittle and any inconsistency in mixing causes a less than satisfactory result. Also the resin is very brittle when set, difficult to cut and will not mould into thin parts very easily. Many small-scale military vehicles were moulded in polyester resin, though manufacturers have almost exclusively turned to polyurethane types.

Opacity, colour and bulk are added to polyester by adding powder, and the resin is made to harden by adding a catalyst

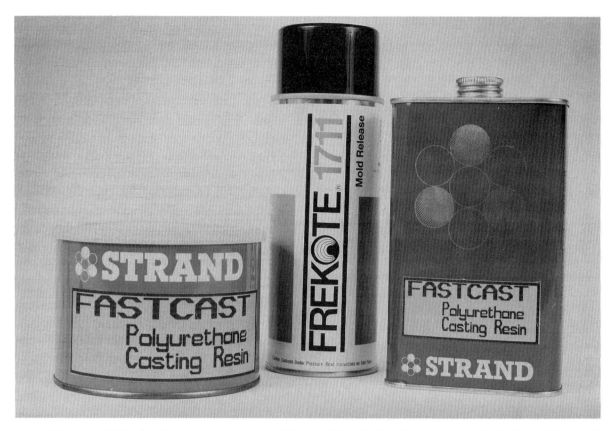

A moulding revolution for the cottage industry and the modeller. Polyurethane resin with Frekote 1711 mould release agent. Polyurethane resins are now widely available and easy to use.

(methyl ethyl ketone peroxide) to the manufacturer's directions.

Polyurethane resins are now more common than polyesters and are much easier to use but, unfortunately, they are more expensive. Polyurethane resins are supplied, normally, as a two-part liquid mix. Both components are roughly the consistency of milk, the resin containing the filler. Normally mixed in 50-50 proportions, and being easy to mix, a type with a short 'pot life' (i.e. before hardening commences) will produce mouldings more quickly and to a higher quality definition than polyester types. Strand Glass make 1 kilogram kits of polyurethane resins designed for home casting purposes.

Resins work better during moulding if some form of 'de-gassing' equipment is available to eliminate air bubbles. Such things are usually beyond the average modeller, and care taken during pouring produces good results. Polyester resins seem to be more prone to air bubbles than polyurethanes, perhaps because of thicker consistencies.

Silicone rubbers of the room temperature vulcanising (RTV) types are ideal for making moulds in which to cast resins. Polyurethane resins are thin enough to spin in centrifugal casting machines, too, and, unlike polyesters, can be drilled carved and stuck together much easier with most contact adhesives.

Metals

All military modellers should familiarise themselves with the metals used for casting model soldiers. These alloys we know colloquially as 'white metals'. Brass and nickel silver etched sheets are now found in model soldier and vehicle kits.

White metal   Used for casting miniature figures in scales 5mm to over 100mm, 'white metal' is derived from the range of soft solders, which are tin/lead alloys with, for figure casting, antimony (in various proportions) added. Small traces of bismuth, copper and zinc can also be found in tin/lead alloys.

The more tin an alloy contains means a better flow and superior definition to those with more lead content, but more tin means more expense and usually higher melting temperatures. Lead is added simply for bulk.

Pewter can be used and is lead-free and rich in tin, but expensive. It moulds well, melting around 245°C, and produces highly detailed castings. Some model figures are cast – as limited runs – in pewter.

Back to white metal, of which there are many different types. It is not unknown for figure manufacturers to use more than one alloy for the same figure kit – the body cast in one type and any weapons (for greater definition on small parts and better strength) in another.

White metals used for casting model soldiers melt, depending on type, in the range 180°C–250°C. Any casting produced should always be carefully cleaned to remove deposits and, because they contain lead, appropriate precautions should be taken when handling, even if it's only the odd white metal figure you assemble and paint.

Brass and nickel silver etched parts   The use of brass and nickel silver parts in the manufacture of white metal and plastic kits is now widespread. Minute brass parts, such as buckles, are etched out of the solid sheet by a photo-chemical process where the original is artwork, drawn many times larger, then reduced and transferred to the metal. The metal is covered with a chemical resist agent over

(exactly) the areas of the part, and then the sheet is immersed in an acid solution where the parts are left as the surrounding area is cut away by the acid. This process is also known as 'chemical milling'.

Metal, in sheet form, is available for modelling purposes in model shop displays under various brand names. Aluminium tube and brass rods, squares, tubes and different sections are all available for the scratchbuilder and converter. A stockpile of useful parts can be built up if a few parts are purchased at each visit.

Wood

Wood is not as widely used as it once was by the military modeller, in conjunction with card or paper, for building miniature vehicles, or for carving master figures. Plastic sheet and two-part epoxy fillers have replaced wood and card. Wood needs finishing before it can be painted – the grain needs filling, otherwise paint just soaks in. However, wood should not be discounted as it is most useful for diorama use, particularly for buildings or interiors in boxed dioramas.

Balsa wood   Most people will be familiar with this lightweight soft wood, which is easy to carve with a sharp knife. A fine-tooth razor saw is best for cutting balsa, especially thicker pieces. Balsa can be glued with balsa cement (cellulose) or PVA and similar water-based adhesives. Balsa can be sanded very easily but its open grain needs sealing before painting.

Jelutong   A light hardwood with an even texture and extremely close grain, jelutong carves beautifully and is a superb modelling medium. It will glue with most adhesives, but does not need as much grain sealing as balsa. Jelutong is not widely available and is expensive compared to other types of wood.

Obeche Heavier than balsa, but still soft with a closer grain and even texture, obeche is very easily carved and sanded, and is a cheaper but stronger alternative to balsa. However, sheet obeche can be split very easily while being worked.

Spruce A stronger wood than obeche, spruce is a close grained softwood which, because of its very straight grain, carves well. Spruce is flexible, and in the solid can be used for complex carvings or producing master parts for mould-making, such as cast armour tank turrets.

Wood must be finished before painting. This can be done using a commercially produced grain-filler, but usually a couple of coats of varnish lightly sanded will suffice on small parts. Do not attempt to achieve saturation, but simply seal the grain. Try carving and experimenting with wood for small parts, for example a wooden crate in miniature can look more realistic in natural wood rather than plastic.

I'm sure many older modellers began their hobby using wood and cardboard and, although such materials have been superseded, they should not be ignored.

Cardboard and paper

While modelling in card is a separate hobby in itself, card and paper can be used in diorama work. For instance, paper, crumpled to 'break' its texture, can be rolled to represent tarpaulins and then coated with diluted PVA glue.

Papers – especially tissue – are good for masking models during spraying or painting. Cards and thicker boards make good concrete slabs for base work. Cut up and positioned to the current pattern, they can also be peeled to produce varying thicknesses. Always use a very sharp knife or scalpel, with a steel straight-edge, and cut on a purpose-built cutting mat or glass plate.

Most glues work on paper and card, from dry-type glue sticks to PVA types. Both can be 'sized' with varnishes to produce a smooth surface for paint. Shellac varnish was previously used for this purpose but varnishes of the polyurethane type work just as well.

Although cardboard has fallen behind the more convenient medium of polystyrene sheet, it should be considered for many tasks where the latter can be a little too 'rigid'.

ADHESIVES

The terms 'adhesives' and 'glue' describe the same thing. There is no real difference but modellers should know the difference between the various types of adhesive especially when using dissimilar materials. What follows is a listing with a description of the more commonly encountered types.

Cyanoacrylates

Also known as 'Super Glues', cyano types have extremely fast setting times and will bond virtually any substances, with few exceptions, one being polythene. There are different types of these glues available now – some with gap-filling properties, quick setting, slower setting, thick and thin types. Accelerators are available as sprays, both aerosol (now with a propellant charge because of harmful CFC gases used previously), and pump operated, which cure the glues almost instantaneously on application. If an excess of adhesive has been applied, when the accelerator is sprayed on, it can and usually does turn the cyanoacrylate white.

Cyanoacrylate will bond skin very easily, so extreme care should be exercised in its use. It can be thinned with 'de-

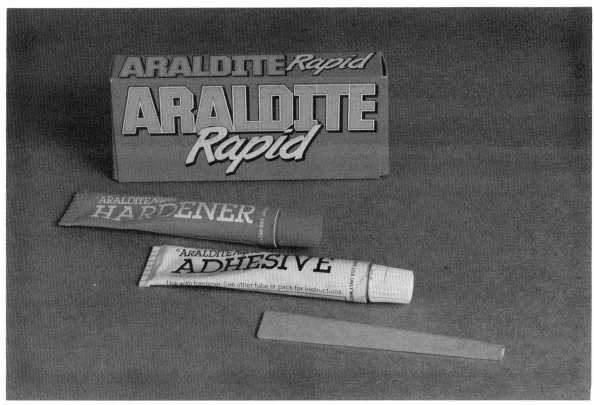

Araldite Rapid two-part epoxy glue. Equal amounts are squeezed from the tube of adhesive and hardener and mixed with the polythene spatula provided. The glue cures in around five minutes with a very tough bond. Slower curing epoxy glues are also available.

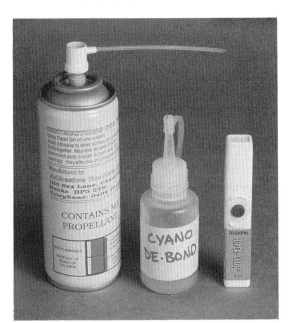

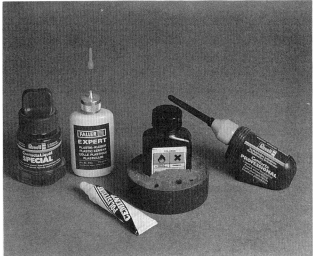

Cyanoacrylate glue, right, works from a pump dispenser by pushing the buttons either side of the container. Always keep the de-bonder near to hand, and clearly labelled when using cyano glues . . . just in case. The can at left contains accelerator for the glue. It contains no propellant, and works by pump action on the white button fitted with a lance.

Plastic glues are numerous. Left to right: Contacta Liquid Special has a thicker viscosity for stronger bonds; Faller Expert, a thicker glue which is dispensed via a very thin metal tube; a small tube of conventional thick polystyrene cement; liquid polystyrene cement in a bottle mounted in Plasticine in a coffee jar lid to stop it falling or being knocked over; Revell Contacta Professional, polystyrene cement dispensed through a thin hollow tube has its protective plastic cover in place.

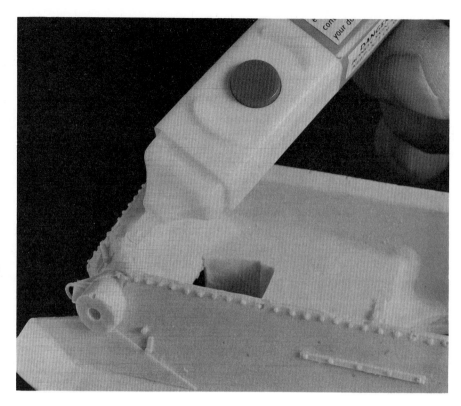

Cyanoacrylate glue, colloquially referred to as 'super glue', is ideal for sticking resins. This dispenser made by Araldite has a pump action (the black button) and a spike in the cap to stop the nozzle clogging and the glue drying up.

bonder' produced for the purpose or with most ladies' nail varnish removers, should any bonding occur which cannot be separated. Acetone-based nail varnish remover is also good for cleaning the tube nozzles after use which can easily clog to the cap, thus rendering the tube useless.

Loctite Super Glue 3 now has a metal rod fitted to the inside of its cap which locates inside the nozzle and eliminates clogging. Containers are now being made in transparent polythene, rather than opaque white, which helps to keep an eye on the level – and also the state – of the contents. Both are moves in the right direction because a large amount of Super Glue is wasted if it is not used within a short space of time.

Polystyrene cements

Available in two basic forms, in a tube or 'liquid' in a bottle for brush application, the adhesive is polystyrene dissolved in solvents. The tube cement can be quite powerful if used excessively, and can melt small parts or distort them. The cements work by dissolving both joining surfaces and, if used correctly, the joint should be very strong.

Liquid cement is much thinner, volatile, yet easy to apply with a small brush. Although it works in the same way as tube glue, its action is not as severe and it 'runs' much better during application. Polystyrene cements can be non-flammable, but solvent vapour from any adhesives should be treated with caution.

Balsa Cement

Not strictly a cement, balsa glue adheres to porous surfaces such as balsa and most woods and other porous surfaces. It will not stick plastic. As far as military modelling is concerned, PVA glues will do the same job and they are cleaner and easier to use.

ABS

Acrylobutyl Styrene plastic needs its own formula adhesive. Remember that most plastics are joined by capillary actions of an adhesive made from particles of the plastic and other additives dissolved in a solvent. ABS 'cement' is no different and it will also bond other plastics, especially polystyrene, though polystyrene cement will not bond ABS plastic with any degree of success.

Most ABS cements are supplied as liquids for brush application and often under trade names such as 'Micro Weld' (from Plastruct).

Acrylic cement

The military modeller will not have much demand for acrylic cement, or Perspex as it is more commonly known, which is specifically designed for bonding acrylic. Acrylic cement contains the basic material – acrylic – dissolved in dichloromethane. Once opened, the cement has a limited shelf life, as do most cements. It is a more virulent substance than polystyrene, and is usually only available from specialist suppliers in quantities far in excess of the modeller's normal requirements.

PVA

Polyvinyl Acetate was designed as a general purpose woodworking glue but it will bond most materials, porous or non-porous, rigid or flexible. It produces a film between the joining surfaces which is quite strong when set. However PVA is water soluble, which can be a disadvantage, but, as far as the military modeller is concerned, this feature can be used to advantage. Diluted PVA can be used to under-coat polythene figures and in ground work for many scenic applications.

PVA dries transparent, although it is white when applied. It will soften after setting if soaked in water. Experiment with this glue whenever possible. It is probably the best adhesive for expanded polystyrene.

Epoxy

Two-part glues, where a hardener is mixed with the adhesive, have been around for quite a long time. Before cyano glues became widely available, epoxies were the modeller's number one choice for sticking white metal figures together. They produce, if mixed and applied correctly, a virtually unbreakable joint.

The two-part glue must be mixed thoroughly and applied to both surfaces. There are many different setting times available, from about five minutes to curing times of over 24 hours. Joints should be supported and clamped while the glue fully sets and cures correctly. The resulting joints will be impervious to water and oil-based paints, and also will have filled any gaps adequately, so lessening any 'soak through' of covering materials – very important on, say, the arm joins on a white metal figure. Excessive adhesive should be cleaned off before setting begins because, once hardened, it is very difficult to remove.

Epoxy glues are thermosetting resin types and their short 'pot life' (i.e. the time the glue starts to set or 'go off') after mixing can be accelerated by heat application. The addition of a hardener at room temperature starts the process, which is irreversible once mixing takes place. Epoxy has good electrical insulation properties and can also be moulded into small parts by the use of one-piece open moulds.

Contact adhesives

General purpose contact glues are extremely useful and there are many different types which all work on the same principle – coat both surfaces with adhesive and allow them to become 'tacky', then press together. Such adhesives produce firm bonds and come ready-mixed in a tube.

Warning Adhesives should always be treated with caution. Do not breathe in any fumes given off, or allow constant exposure or contact on the skin, because

	Polystyrene	Expanded Polystyrene	Polyester Resin	Polyurethane Resin	ABS Plastic	Acrylic (Perspex)	Balsa, Soft & Hard Woods	Card & Paper	White Metal
White Metal	C G	B	C G	C G	C G	C G	G	C G	C G
Card & Paper	B GH	B	G	G H	C G	C G	BF GH	BC GH	
Balsa, Soft & Hard Woods	B GH	B	G	G	G	G	BF GH		
Acrylic (Perspex)	E	B	C G	CE G	CE G	E			
ABS Plastic	D	B	C G	CD EG	D				
Polyurethane Resin	A	B	C G	A					
Polyester Resin	CE G	B	C G						
Expanded Polystyrene	B	B							
Polystyrene	A								

A. Polystyrene cement
B. PVA cement
C. Cyanoacrylates ('Super Glues')
D. ABS cement
E. Acrylic cement
F. Balsa cement
G. Epoxy glues
H. Contact adhesives

they contain irritants. Do not sniff vapours as this can cause respiratory and brain damage.

Use the simple table on p46 as a guide to which adhesives will bond dissimilar materials. It will be found that cyano-acrylates, for example, will bond most of those materials listed, although it has not been listed for the majority. Cyano-acrylates do not normally work well on porous material, however, though constant applications will build up a 'seal' until bonding is made possible *via* saturation of the material's fibres.

Used carefully, and for tasks for which they were intended, adhesives are a boon. Abused they can be, at worst, killers. Keep them away from children, and locked away at all times when not in use. Always use adhesives, whatever their type, in a well-ventilated area, avoid eye and skin contact and always follow the manufacturers' instructions carefully.

PAINTS

Water-soluble paints

Water colours Basic water colour paints are available in tubes and pans (blocks), are water-soluble bound with gum arabic, and are only really good for absorbent papers. They are applied in transparent washes, are weak in colour and dry to a matt finish. They can be used for small details on figures and vehicle models painted over other colours and are worth experimenting with.

Gouache Also known as 'designer's colours', gouache paints are supplied in tubes but lack the luminosity and transparency of water colours. The paints dry to a matt finish and lighten as they dry out. They can be used carefully over a matt white oil enamel undercoat on figures, but they will not stand any handling, no

Maestro Craft colours. These acrylic paints have a slower drying time than conventional acrylic paint and can be blended if the painter works quickly.

matter how careful. Natural skin oils from the fingers can destroy any painted surface quite easily.

Poster paint Supplied in tube, pot and powder form, poster paint is opaque when applied. Like gouache and water colour, poster colour is thinned with water. It can be used on figures suitably undercoated with white enamel.

Casein added to water-soluble paints, combined with a finely ground pigment is marketed as 'Plaka' by the Pelikan Company of Germany. Plaka dries perfectly matt and is a popular choice for some figure painters. However, it must be worked very quickly because of its quick drying rate. Being finely pigmented, Plaka sprays through the airbrush very easily once thinned and strained before use and has good adhesive properties.

Acrylics Acrylic paints have become very popular in modelling circles in recent years. Although they can be thinned with water, their solvent base is ethyl alcohol and they come in tubes or pots, the latter being specifically designed for modellers. Intensity of colour and opacity are very good and by using additives the finish can be controlled through from matt to full gloss.

Once hard, acrylics are difficult to shift and so brushes and utensils must be cleaned with water immediately after use. Acrylics spray through the airbrush very easily, but it is recommended that solvent should be used for any final 'blowing through' after a spraying session.

Emulsion Similar in consistency to acrylics, emulsion paints are intended for household use. However, they have good properties and the modeller can use them for scenic work. Crown Paints (as well as other makers) produce 'Matchpots', small, sample-size quantities of emulsion in a

small pot for a relatively small sum, and these are suitable for military modelling. Although intended for DIY decorators to experiment with, there are a lot of colours to choose from. Although all shades are not suitable, they can be mixed and adapted with a little imagination. Also, like acrylic, they cover expanded polystyrene very well.

Oil-based paints

Enamels Enamels are the best-known modellers' paints and are available in tins, bottles and aerosol spray cans. The thinner is turpentine or white spirit. Colour availability is extensive, and there are many shades produced specifically for military modellers. There are different theories governing how enamels should be applied, and experimentation is advised. Use with airbrushes presents no problem, so long as the paint is well stirred then thinned and strained correctly.

Humbrol market specially thinned enamels for the airbrush in quite a sizeable range of colours. Metallic enamels are quite easy to use but, unless sprayed on, can leave brush marks over large areas. Enamels are available in matt, semi-matt, or 'eggshell' and gloss.

Oils Oil paints are the favoured medium for many figure painters. They are supplied in tubes and are designed for picture painting, but have been adapted by modellers and are most popular for painting figures which have been suitably undercoated, usually with flat enamel. Being totally intermixable, they can be blended and worked for long periods before even beginning to dry out. Some can, in time, fade or yellow, so it's best to learn of their capabilities before use. Most oil paints dry out to give a slight sheen.

For figure painting, 'Artists' Quality'

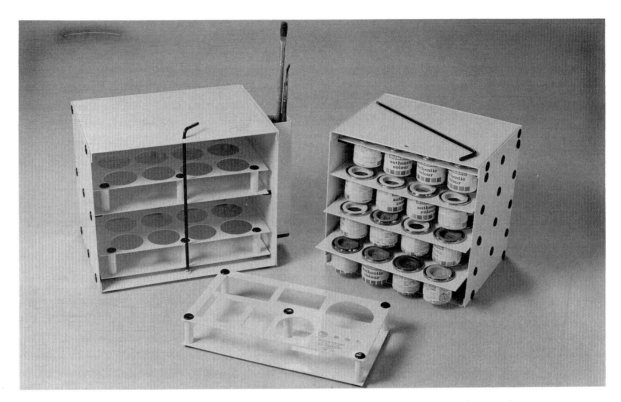

Storage boxes for tins of enamel paint – easy to transport, the paint can't spill and everything is tidy. These units are made by Southford Products.

must be used. Any lesser qualities do not have such finely ground pigments and can be too coarse for use.

Oil paints are thinned with turpentine or linseed oil and other specialist additives are available. The use of linseed oil for painting miniatures is discouraged, as its addition produces too much oil, the colours take longer to dry out and the matt effect ideally required is somewhat lessened.

Alkyd colours Winsor and Newton produce Alkyd colours which are, like oils, pure pigments, but ground in alkyd resin. They can be treated with the same materials and thinned with turpentine. Drying time is shorter than oil paints but petroleum distillate will retard the drying time of alkyd colours. Alkyd resins are synthetics derived from alcohols and acids.

Cellulose-based paints

Cellulose paints will melt some plastics –

especially polystyrene – and so they are not popular with military modellers, despite their suitability for painting white metal.

Available in tins, bottles and aerosols, cellulose is best applied over a self-etch primer on metals after they have been 'degreased'.

ABS plastic will take cellulose, although polystyrene can 'melt'. However, if sprayed on in very thin coats, polystyrene can be covered. But why bother when enamels are less trouble?

Preparation and priming ready for painting

All materials should be prepared before the first brush is dipped into the paint, or the airbrush charged. Plastics, depending on the paint used, usually need a primer, as do woods and metals.

Plastic All plastics should first be

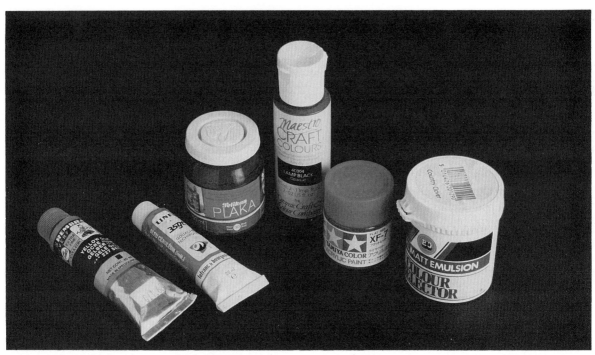

A selection of paint containers, left to right: Talens Rembrandt artist quality oil paint in a tube. Designers' gouache in a tube. Plaka in a jar with plastic snap-on cap. Maestro acrylic in its distinctive container. Tamiya acrylic in a jar. An emulsion tester sold in DIY stores is a valuable source of acrylic type paint for diorama builders . . . a source the modeller should investigate.

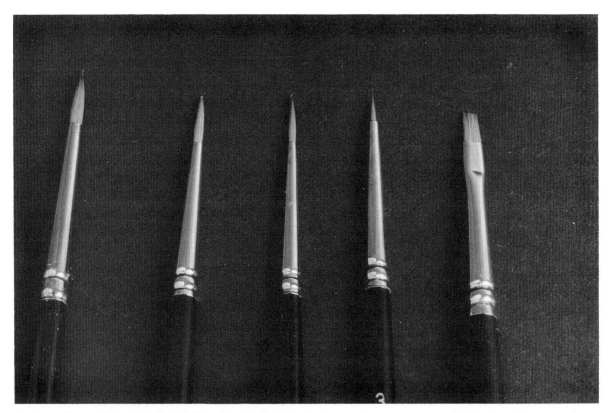

Good quality sable brushes last a long time if cared for. Left to right are: Nos. 2, 1, 00, 000 and an O flat made by a German manufacturer and one of a batch bought by me for a very reasonable sum at Kulmbach Model Figure Börse in Bavaria some years ago. Lay in stocks whenever you can, they're always needed.

washed in warm water and mild detergent. Injection-moulded plastic kit parts can carry remnants of mould release agents, which, although invisible to the naked eye, will impair paint adhesion. After assembly and filling, you should wash the completed model and allow it to dry naturally. Do not touch the surface with your fingers, otherwise grease deposits will be transferred to it no matter how clean your hands are.

If you are using oil paints on a plastic figure, first prime the surface with matt enamel and use white or a shade complementary to the top colour to provide a 'tooth' for the oil paint. With enamels or acrylics, it is unnecessary to prime the surface.

Polythene figures, after washing, should be primed with thin coats of diluted PVA glue which will dry to a hard shell and thus accept most paints. If using oils, undercoat with matt enamel.

Expanded polystyrene can be primed with thin coats of acrylic paints lightly sanded between each coat until the surface is sealed. The final coating of acrylic will form a plastic shell, enabling even enamels which would otherwise melt expanded polystyrene to be safely applied.

Metal Any fluxes used for soldering should be removed with solvents and the figure or parts washed in warm soapy water. Similar treatment should be given to assemblies that have been glued. Scrub clean with toothbrush, then buff up, if possible, with a fine wire brush in a miniature power tool, then wash again ready for priming.

Metal must be primed to prevent any oxidisation taking effect later. Self-etch cellulose primers or polyurethane varnishes are ideal. Finish by priming with matt enamel as a key for painting.

Wood You should seal the wood grain and sand the surface, or the paint will not form a fine smooth surface nor sink into the wood. Wood fillers are available which seal the grain with more than one coat, sanding between each. When the wood is smooth, prime with an undercoat before brushing or spraying the finishing coats. Multiple coats of polyurethane varnish can be used as a grain filler on most woods.

Card and paper Cardboard is easily sealed with varnish. Shellac used to be the one for the job, but polyurethane varnish is better. After coating, sand and then prime for painting. Paper can be soaked in diluted PVA glue and allowed to dry, where it will set with a plastic coating which will readily accept paint. This is good for making tarpaulins and bed rolls out of paper for AFV models.

Fillers

Most kits and figurines usually require some sort of gap filler necessitated by mould shrinkage or badly designed parts. All gaps must be filled before painting.

Plastic fillers Available in tubes, these fillers 'attack' polystyrene surfaces and, if not used with care, can ruin a model's surface. They should be applied sparingly and in stages. Some can shrink during curing ... some worse than others.

Plastic Padding (used for car repairs) is useful for filling large gaps, and can be used for filling balsa wood parts for a smooth finish, such as found on cast parts on model AFVs.

Epoxy fillers, the most popular in the UK being Milliput, are now indispensable. Masters for figurines are made in Milliput because, once hardened, it can be carved, drilled, sanded and shaped with engraving tools.

Epoxy fillers are two-part compounds –

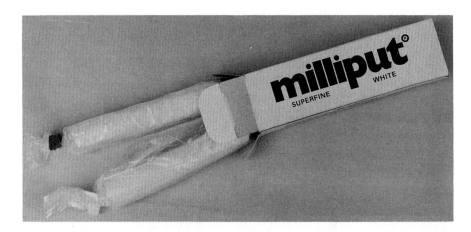

Milliput two-part epoxy
putty.

filler and hardener – which, when mixed, form a putty-like dough which will eventually harden. The cure rate can be accelerated with heat and the surface smoothed before curing with water or moistened tools.

Polyfilla and Tetrion　Made for DIY home repairs and decorating, Polyfilla, especially the fine surface type, has many applications. Also known as 'spackling paste', it sticks to plastic well, and to a lesser degree to white metal. It is most useful for basework on single figure displays or vignettes. Diluted it can be used for 'rendering' the walls of model buildings. It can be coloured with powder paint pigments before application.

Tetrion is a harder plaster very good for representing rough stonework on model buildings. It is a very effective wood grain sealer.

Low-melt solders　Solder has a gap-filling property and, once the art of soldering is mastered for figures and vehicles, all joints can be filled during construction, or if preferred, at a later stage. It can also be used to build up detail on white metal figures and is most helpful for conversions.

Brushes

Brushes are an essential part of the mili-

tary modeller's kit. Only the best sables should be purchased for figure painting because cheaper types, whatever their attraction, will not give the required result. Red Kolinsky Sables are expensive, but probably the best. Experimentation will show which suits you best; some modellers prefer smaller brushes with short hairs, while others go for longer bristles with a fine point. Examine the brushes before you buy.

Always keep your brushes scrupulously clean. After thorough cleaning with the appropriate solvent, wash them in warm soapy water and 'reform' the bristles and store upright in a pot with the bristles protected with a tube. Try not to mix your brushes, and if possible, use one set for oil, another for acrylic, etc. This way, brush life will be prolonged.

For scenic work and much vehicle model work, consider cheaper brushes for the overall application of colour if you do not have access to an airbrush.

Aerosol sprays　As an alternative to brush painting, aerosols are suitable for covering large areas and are useful for undercoating, especially on model figurines and vehicles where thin coats are possible, thus not obscuring any fine detail. Paint will deteriorate in aerosols and the can must be shaken thoroughly for at least two minutes before spraying. After use invert

A Micon oil-less diaphragm compressor with Badger single-action airbrushes.

the can and spray to clear the nozzle. If possible, use an aerosol entirely in one spraying and always use it in a well-ventilated area.

Airbrushes An airbrushed finish, correctly applied, is far superior to one made with a brush. However, a good airbrush is not cheap and neither is the compressor that powers it. Aerosol cans are available to power airbrushes, but this is an expensive exercise. Airbrushing is a technique in itself and beyond the scope of this book. If possible, watch an airbrush in use, or ask for a demonstration of the equipment and have a try yourself.

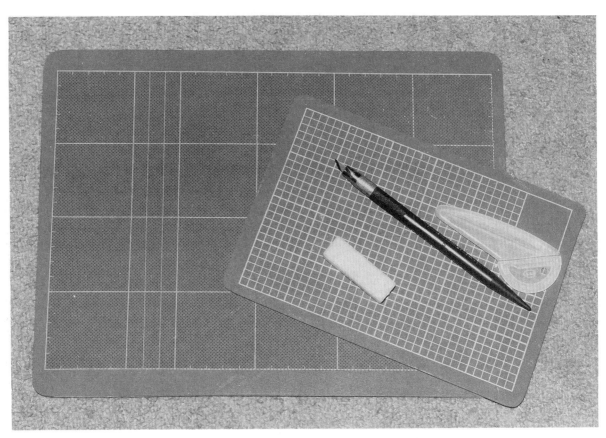

A good cutting out board of the modern 'self-sealing' plastic type is not cheap, but it lasts indefinitely and will protect any surface from becoming cut and marked by modelling knives. Some are printed with horizontal and vertical grid markings as an aid to marking out.

CHAPTER 4

MINIATURE FIGURINES

Collectors of miniature figurines fall, generally, into two groups: those who assemble and paint figures, and those who convert and scratchbuild – painters and modellers.

The high standard of commercial figurines today leaves very little for the painter/collector to do, except assemble, prime and paint. However, the figure modeller will still convert, adapt and scratchbuild from 'spares' or completely from scratch, doing all the sculpture from the armature upwards.

In figure competitions, there are often different categories or classes to differentiate between painted-only figures and scratchbuilt or conversions. Often the reverse is the case and, when a scratchbuilt figure competes against a painted commercial figure, the judge should take into account the 'work done' on the model and not just that it's 'a good paint job!' Simple categories are necessary for fairness.

The competition system used in the UK simply defines the category into which figures should be entered, and is intended to give everyone a fair chance against the standard set by the quality of entries overall. The overall 'standard' can only be determined by the models entered on any particular occasion, and not by any one person setting a criteria to judge to!

FLAT FIGURES

The flat figure is a two-dimensional miniature, and the most popular scale is for 30mm-tall figures although larger ones

A Roman officer – 30mm flat figure from Doste of Germany.

Flats come in all sizes . . . the smaller ones here are 30mm whilst the figure on his horse (Christian IV of Denmark) measures around 120mm to the top of his plume!

Flats are aptly named and . . . flat, as illustrated by the one held in the hand which is a 30mm figure the same as that at right which is included for scale.

are available. Traditionally the figures were, and some still are, cast in slate moulds which are two-piece assemblies and have both halves hand-engraved by the sculptor. Being two-dimensional, the figure shows both front and back detail. This is not always finished on both sides at the painting stage if the figure is to be displayed in a frame with only one side showing – a common form of display.

If both sides are visible, then, of course, both should be painted. Painting flats is akin to painting a picture, and skill is needed to make a one-dimensional object appear round, with relief. Also, the work is precise because of the scale when the figures are only 30mm high. A flats painter must, indeed, be skilled in the use of the brush and know the capabilities of his paints thoroughly. Flats are usually displayed 'flat' in a display frame on a single-colour background. They can also be utilised in a diorama form on an open base, or in a boxed diorama with artificial lighting. Whatever the display feature, flats are best viewed directly onto the side, at perfect right-angles, otherwise the illusion is lost.

Although flats are mostly cast in white metal, injection-moulded plastic (polystyrene) ones were produced in France some years ago. Some of these were semi-round too, and not perfectly 'flat'. Flats have also been cast in metal in centrifugal casting machines, a far cry from the traditional slate moulds.

Little can be done, nor, perhaps, should be, in converting flats, as they are intended purely as 'painters' figures'. Traditionally, they are painted with artists' oils to make possible the subtle blending needed to create the illusion in highlight and shade. However, some painters do excellent work using enamels or acrylic paint, so it's worth experimenting with these mediums to check their suitability to your own taste.

Colours must be kept bright and precise on flat figures. It's no use allowing them to become muddy in appearance, otherwise the precise colour values and effects needed will be destroyed.

For the modeller, flats are not really expensive. Considering the amount of time needed to paint one, and the enjoyment gained as entertainment value, they are unbeatable. However, make no mistake about it, figure painting should be regarded as a pastime and fun, and never the chore that some people seem to make it.

Painting flats

If you can join a military modelling club that has flat figure painters amongst its membership – join it! The best way to learn about painting flats (and any figures for that matter) is to be shown by someone who is willing to give you a practical demonstration. Hands-on practice under supervision is the best way to learn.

First the casting must be examined and cleaned or fettled. With flat figures it's usually metal flash that needs removing – this is excess metal which has seeped between the mould halves during casting and has caused the joining of various details by forming webs between them.

Undercoat the flat (either on one or both sides, the choice is up to the painter) with matt white paint, enamel or cellulose, by brush or spray. The airbrush gives a particularly fine micro-thin coat of paint. A piece of very thick card with a slit cut in it will secure the flat when its narrow base is slotted into it. The flat can be painted held by the card after the undercoat has thoroughly dried out. Your colour values will vary if the card you use is black, white, grey, light brown or whatever, so it's worth experimenting again. Modelling

Optional legs! and this only applies to flats. With this three-legged individual you can take your choice. Remove one of the right legs for a walking or running pose.

Undercoating in matt white enamel or acrylic not only provides a good key for the painting stage but also shows up any flaws. Two small blow holes are evident in the horse's flank just behind the rear end of the saddle cloth. They must be filled and re-undercoated before painting can commence.

is 90% experimentation after all! (see colour sections).

Painting a flat is like painting a picture. You have to decide where the light is coming from and paint light and shade to suit – including shadows! If your first attempts do not please you, simply clean off the paint (very easy with oil paints) and start again. This is one of the major advantages of the oil medium in figure painting when compared to other types of paints, and therefore it is recommended that oils, despite their mystique, are used from the word go.

ROUND FIGURES

Round figures, in any scale, moulded in white metal or plastic, are extremely popular with military modellers. Regarded by many as a three-dimensional art form, a well-painted miniature figurine is a joy to behold and does invite attention and interest from anyone who appreciates such artistry. They can also command a high price from collectors, but more often it's the casual observer who is fascinated, and who is so taken with the painted miniature that another military modeller is born. A lot of people look, admire and then want to have a go themselves. It's a well-known fact that most military modellers began their hobby by admiring the work of others.

Round figures, in the main, are usually extremely well made and detailed. Cast in plastic, resin or, most commonly, in white metal, there is a large selection to choose from in scales ranging from 30mm to around 120mm high, of which 54mm, 75mm and 90mm are the most popular sizes, or scales. The range of resin figure kits 120mm high from Belgian manufacturer Verlinden Productions has become very popular in the past few years.

In 54mm scale, the 'traditional' size, modellers are fortunate enough to have

Round figures. These are 54mm modern Israeli Defence Force, a WWII German and US Military Policeman from Verlinden Productions.

Left: simple 1:32 scale polystyrene figures from the Elastolin range by Preiser of Germany. These figures can easily be converted and modified. *Bottom*: 1:32 scale civilians of the Victorian era, sold as a set and ready painted. Again, they show good conversion potential and can even be converted and pressed into military service!

plenty of separate parts available from which to *make* figures, not just assemble and paint kits. This is also becoming true for other scales, as manufacturers realise there is also a market in converting what they produce and which it would be foolish to ignore.

Plastic figures became widely available in the 1950s and were initially moulded in polythene. They were intended as toys, and are still regarded as such, perhaps wrongly, by some modellers. The moulded detail on these figures was very good and superior to anything on the market at that time. Many modellers would have preferred the figures to have been moulded in the more rigid polystyrene, but it was to be some years before Historex of France and

Airfix in the UK mass-produced figure kits in this type of plastic, causing an instant 'boom' in the hobby. Soft polythene type figures were not aimed at modellers and collectors, but at the toy market, especially youngsters. However, as with most things produced as toys, modellers have learned to convert, adapt and utilise just about anything they can get their hands on.

It is not unknown for modellers to mix their mediums when it comes to converting and scratchbuilding. Some white metal figures have received plastic heads, just as metal heads have been put onto plastic bodies, and some very attractive and competent models have been produced in this way.

Painting fully round figures is really a matter of taste. Many words have been exchanged over what is the best paint, how to apply it, which additives should be used, and so on. In the end, experimentation on the modeller's part is the key. By all means, copy styles at first, but adapt and, where possible, improve on your first efforts. Practice *does* make perfect as far as painting military miniatures is concerned.

PLASTIC FIGURES

Plastic figures are moulded in expensive multi-unit steel moulds fed with molten plastic under great pressure enabling mass production, whereas white metal figures, as far as the model figure market is concerned, are cast in hardened vulcanised rubber moulds spun on a centrifugal casting machine. Both systems need a master figure, or pattern, to begin with – only the form of casting and the material used are different. Some plastic kits are produced from limited run production moulds made of a composition material good for about 30 – 40,000 castings to keep tooling costs down.

Plastic master figures or patterns are

A Historex standard bearer built straight from the packet . . . with no additions or frills!

usually designed to a much larger scale than the finished product, and can be pantographed down to scale and cut into the steel mould or by spark erosion in some cases.

Figures cast in white metal alloys from vulcanised rubber moulds are produced normally from same-size masters, the process being not entirely different from injection moulding, but slightly less technical as far as machine tools are concerned.

The cost of producing tooled steel-injection moulds nowadays is very expensive and seems to have become confined to countries in the East, such as Taiwan and Korea where production costs for new models are much less than in Western countries. Manufacturers now 'rotate' moulds so many kits can be marketed under different brand names, which is not only good for the modeller but enables a much wider field of marketing for the manufacturer.

Plastic figures are preferred by many modellers, as they are easier and more convenient to work than white metal. Plastic (except polythene) sticks easily and can be cut, filed and bent to different configurations.

At the time of writing, the largest range of plastic figures is that produced by the French company Historex, although, unfortunately, new additions to this company's range seem to have dried up somewhat. The company has now gone into 'Judicial Receivership' in France. The

Airfix ranges of 'Multipose' and 'Collectors Series' are once again available, and this company's polythene figures are still widely sold in chain stores and hobby shops. These ranges are nominally described as 54mm, but the Historex range is 1:30 scale and Airfix 1:32 scale. The theory has been put forward that one (Historex) type was measured from the around to eye level and the other to the top of the head! People are different in shape and thus it is much easier to work things out as a ratio. Historex figures certainly need treatment to 'humanise' them and modify their upright stance if they are simply assembled from the kit of parts supplied.

Polythene figures

Polythene figures can be painted, but first they must be washed in warm water and

A new wave of multi-pose figures from Dragon to 1:35 scale. There's sufficient for four different figures for a very reasonable outlay.

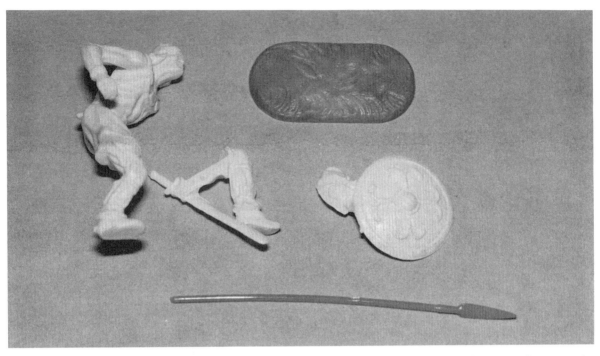

An Elastolin figure by Preiser consisting of only five parts. With work this dark age figure can become quite acceptable considering the figure is intended for the toy market. The bent plastic spear would be best replaced.

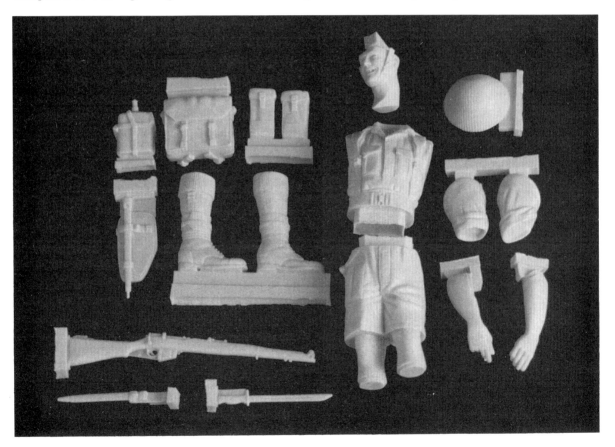

Components that make up a 120mm Verlinden Productions figure. The parts are cast in polyurethane resin, in one piece moulds indicated by the moulding plugs to which they are attached. This moulding process gives no mould part lines on the pieces. The blocks or resin plugs must be carefully removed with razor saw and knife, finishing with fine grade emery paper.

detergent (washing-up liquid is good for this) to remove any surface grease and mould release agents, and then cleaned up by removing the mould separation marks which will be found going right round the figure. These cannot be filed nor sanded away; polythene is far too 'oily' in texture for this. A really sharp blade (such as a brand new scalpel blade) is necessary to pare away carefully any ridges and flash. Straight cuts only should be made; do not make a scraping action with the knife and be careful not to cut into the plastic because it cannot be filled with putty to any degree of success. The surface must be treated to accept and retain the paint. Polythene will not take paint directly onto its surface with any permanence but, if the figure is treated with water-diluted PVA glue, a greater degree of success is possible.

Paint the diluted PVA glue (Unibond is an old favourite for this process) over the figure. Two thin coats are better than one thick one, and allow it to dry out into a hard thin shell which shrinks over the figure, enabling undercoating and painting along conventional lines to be carried out.

Conversion of polythene figures does present problems. As mentioned earlier, polythene is one of the groups of 'unstickable' plastics and thus any arms or body halves must be pinned for strength before coating with diluted PVA glue. Experiments have shown that cyanoacrylate glues may 'hold' polythene, though not, it appears, with any permanence. Any texturing, such as hair, can be worked with a pyrogravure, though care must be taken because mistakes are not easily rectified.

Polystyrene figures

Hard polystyrene figures are easy to assemble, detail, prime and paint. Assembly with a polystyrene cement could not be easier, and polystyrene does not have any of the disadvantages of its stablemate polythene.

After washing all parts in warm water and mild detergent to remove the usual surface deposits, you can remove any mould part lines with knife and file. When assembling a figure from a kit, I recommend a 'dry run' to ensure the fit of parts. Plastic of the polystyrene type does not require priming, but a coat of matt enamel is advised to give a 'tooth' to any paint used to finish and to show up discrepancies on the figure's surface. Do not use cellulose-based auto-primers on polystyrene: it sometimes works if the spray is misted onto the plastic, but there can be a reaction and, at worst, the moulded detail on the surface may be completely destroyed. Enamels and acrylics can be painted onto polystyrene without an undercoat.

Polystyrene figures are good for converting and quite interesting types can be made up from spare parts such as bodies, legs, arms, heads, etc., to produce a figure not available as a kit. Of course, uniform distinctions will have to be added from modelling materials or adapted from the parts.

Further animation is possible by cutting arms and legs and repositioning them. Bodies can be twisted and heads turned, raised to look up or lowered to look down. Polystyrene can be worked with the pyrogravure; details such as hair, fur trimming on uniforms, head-dress plumes, horses' manes and tails will benefit from careful modelling with this useful instrument. After modelling is completed, the figure should, once again, be washed in warm water and mild detergent solution before undercoating (if required) and painting.

Modelling in polystyrene, using spare parts from Historex or Airfix 'Multipose' for example, limits the builder to 54mm (1:32 scale) or to 1:35 scale from the growing number of plastic figure kits.

Larger figures, 1:12 scale from Airfix and Tamiya (a single 1:9 scale figure from ESCI) can be adapted easily too. Tamiya's racing driver and pit crew figures will be found to be somewhat short in stature, but some excellent conversions have been made with them as they are reasonably priced and easy to work, being of hollow construction. During conversion, any alteration of stature and height can be made to give the subject figure some individuality and, perhaps, better anatomy.

A large 200mm scale WWII German soldier from Verlinden Productions illustrates the many extra pieces of equipment included with figures today.

Resin figures

Polyurethane resin moulded figures are now available worldwide from quite a few manufacturers. The resin has similar working properties to polystyrene but is much harder, and cyanoacrylate glue is one of the best adhesives to assemble kit parts. Polyurethane resin gives high definition castings and will show the slightest flaw on the master. Carelessly moulded, it can produce a lot of air bubble marks on the surface of the model. Milliput filler can be used effectively on polyurethane resin models.

Verlinden Productions of Belgium is probably the largest maker of polyurethane resin figures in both 1:35 scale and also an expanding range of figure kits 120mm high. The series offers mainly World War Two and modern subjects but also a good range with conversion potential. Accessory ranges of heads, hands, arms and equipment are available too, which broadens the scope for conversions quite a lot.

WHITE METAL FIGURES

'White metal' figures are, usually, cast in hardened or vulcanised rubber moulds on centrifugal casting machines. The alloys used basically comprise lead, tin and bismuth, and are melted down in thick-walled melting pots, usually with some form of temperature control, and poured in a molten state into the spinning mould on the centrifuge. Depending upon the skill of the pattern and mould-makers, a high definition casting results, but it is this skill in both fields that separates a good figure from a bad one.

White metal figures can be even more detailed than their plastic counterparts and have sharper and more defined details. They are certainly heavier, but they do cost more because of the very nature of their production and the materials used in their manufacture. However, for what you get they represent good value for money, and when painted up . . . well, that's another story!

A lot of modellers will shrink from converting a metal figure although they will 'leap into action' on a plastic one, wielding the modelling knife with infinite dexterity. However, converting metal figures is not really difficult – it just takes more time and a lot more care, especially when the cost is fresh in your memory as you reach for the saw.

This is the reason why so many similar metal figures are seen in competition, modellers preferring to paint rather than convert to be just that little bit different. Although there is on the surface nothing wrong with this concept, it does limit creativity to some degree. If you have any intention of entering competitions, it is well to bear this in mind.

White metal figures are normally very easy to assemble if the job is not rushed and every care is taken. Glues, such as epoxy resin and cyanoacrylate types, will do the job admirably but these figures can also be soldered together with the special low-melt solders that are available, using a temperature-controlled soldering iron.

White metal figures can range from a one-piece casting with only the base to add, to quite complicated kits where the military modeller has to assemble everything himself. The excellently produced kits by master modeller Ray Lamb, in his Poste Militaire range, spring to mind, offering the modeller complexity and finesse of casting previously not thought possible. Imagine for example, a complete harness for a horse in a 90mm white metal kit!

The modeller should always first wash white metal figure castings in warm water and mild detergent, by totally immersing all the castings and then giving them a good scrub with an old toothbrush, ensuring it gets into every nook and cranny. This procedure is necessary, and more so than with plastic figures, to neutralise and remove any mould release agents still adhering to castings. When all has been done, rinse and blot dry with soft paper tissue or allow to dry naturally. Try not to handle the figure too much until after assembly.

The next stage is to remove any flash and mould part lines. If the mould in which the figure was cast is good and the caster knows his business, then there should be no 'flash' on the castings at all. 'Flash' is caused by a badly-fitting mould where the metal flows from the cavity between the faces of the mould producing a 'membrane'; for instance between a figure's legs.

The standards achieved in figure casting have virtually eliminated 'flash' completely but, if it is evident, remove it with a knife and files.

Mould parting lines, however, are virtually 'hair lines' on a good figure and much worse on a not-so-good figure. They are the result of the contour of the joint lines of the two-piece mould where it follows the natural break, or part, line around the figure to eliminate any 'undercuts'. Undercuts, of course, would not allow the figure to be easily removed from the mould, and are therefore eliminated by the mould-maker by routing the mould part line in the most convenient position. More thought goes into mould-making today – previously standards were lower and it was common to find a mould part line centrally down a figure's face causing terrible distortion, and also proving very difficult to remove without destroying much of the facial detail, the main attraction of any figure. Now these are made laterally, across the head and behind the ears. Also, where possible, heads are

Above: components of a simple 54mm white figure kit from New Hope Design. *Below right*: removing the mould part lines with a needle file.

final 'touching in' with paint where the joints appear.

Glued assembly for white metal figures is by far the most popular method among modellers. However, some modellers do prefer soldered assembly and this will be discussed later as a guide to those versed in the practice of soldering in other spheres.

Epoxy resins are the most suitable adhesives for white metal figure kits. Two varieties are commercially available – the 'normal set' and a 'quick set' or 'five-minute' epoxy. Whichever you choose, always read and follow very carefully the manufacturer's instructions for mixing the glue. Also, always ensure that bonding surfaces are scrupulously clean. Fine cross hatching with a knife blade does aid adhesion and should be done whenever possible, especially on flat, butting surfaces.

A thin layer on both surfaces to be joined is made with a tiny spatula or a wooden

moulded separately for greater flexibility in production.

Mould hair lines can be scraped away with a knife and finished off with a needle file. Care must be taken to ensure that no detail is obscured during this operation, and that any fine work incorporated by the pattern-maker is not obliterated by the careless application of simple hand tools.

When all parts have been cleaned up, assembly can begin. However, before reaching for the glue or soldering iron, it must be determined – especially with kits of many components – just how much will be obscured and inaccessible to the paint-brush after final assembly. If any parts fit this category, and after a dry assembly run it will become clear which these are, they should be set aside and primed and painted separately, to be added later to the main casting when all paint is dry, leaving only

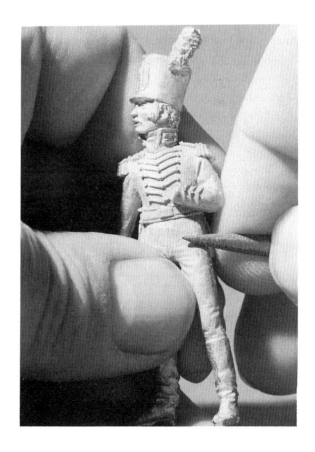

cocktail stick; the latter can get into all areas, such as the locating holes for arm spigots. When the pieces are brought together they should be supported, clamped or wired where possible – or both! Leave the glued parts until the adhesive cures thoroughly, but ensure that any excess glue that may have oozed from the joints is wiped away. Its removal later may prove rather difficult.

Heat will accelerate the setting time of epoxy whereas cold slows it down somewhat. Do not, however, put white metal figures near direct heat sources such as cooker grills or place them in a domestic oven. While this *can* be done successfully, some modellers ignorant of the low melting point of white metal have reduced prized figures to pools of molten metal. If an oven is used, the figure should be suspended somehow or mounted on a block of wood, but not on a metal tray which will conduct all available heat and thus melt the figure.

If you're anxious to see a completed model, use the 'five-minute' epoxy which does not give as much positioning time for tricky parts, but does 'go off' pretty fast when compared with the regular variety, whose pot time can be quite extended depending on conditions.

Epoxy bonds are virtually unpartable. Cyanoacrylates or 'super glues' (to give their popular name, based on one of the first commercial trade marks) will stick to white metal quite well. Their use is quick and clean and, above all, convenient. Although they possess initially as much strength as epoxy, experience has shown that rough handling can cause parts to drop off figures after some time, and certainly larger joints can fail under pressure. A sharp blow, or if the model is dropped, can cause cyano glues to 'shear' especially if the joint had not been a clean one. It's also not unknown for the glue to crack from the results of bad handling. The many modellers wielding tubes of 'super glue' at competitions, repairing models 'broken in transit' is testimony to this.

As with most products, improvements to cyano-type adhesives have been made since their widespread commercial introduction. There are newer types on the market with gap-filling properties, which do work quite well and also accelerators that make the glue go off virtually immediately, in easy spray form, and even non-aerosol pump dispensers which are environmentally friendly as far as the lack of harmful propellant gases are concerned. Accelerators can, however, turn any exposed cyano glue white and powdery, and this deposit cannot be removed easily from the model's surface without a special debonding agent. Extra thin and cyanos especially formulated for plastic are also available. One day, perhaps, they'll have one for polythene – but it seems unlikely!

'Super glues' are extra-thin and can ooze out of joints and run down the model very easily if care is not taken, so apply them sparingly. Also, watch your fingers; skin can be bonded to the model figure very easily. Debonders are available that will neutralise the adhesive and ensure a 'clean' and painless parting where skin is concerned. Debonders can also be used to clean surplus glue away from delicate joints.

Soldered joints

As an alternative to adhesives, soldering is not really difficult for figure construction. That said, however, many beginners would not agree and many would also not even attempt to solder a figure together at all. The only equipment needed is a temperature-controlled soldering iron, the low-melt solder and the correct flux for the job.

There are, basically, two methods of joining parts together on white metal figures

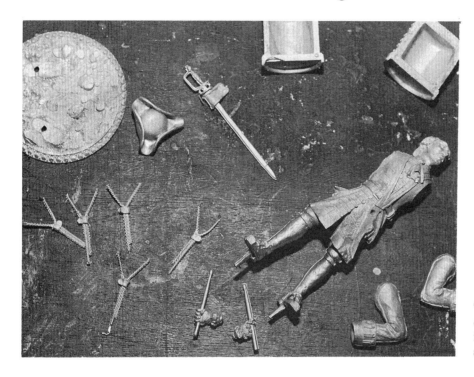

The parts of a Hinchliffe drummer laid out ready for a soldered assembly session.

– direct application of the solder and soldering iron together on a fluxed joint, and sweating the components together to produce a neat and automatically-filled joint. As with glue, all mating surfaces must be clean, but on white metal it helps if they are first burnished with a wire brush. This offers a superbly shiny surface for excellent flux dispersion and adhesion.

The flux is all-important in soldering. The solder will not flow in the joints where flux is not present; it simply forms globules and will not disperse correctly. Direct application of iron and solder to suitable

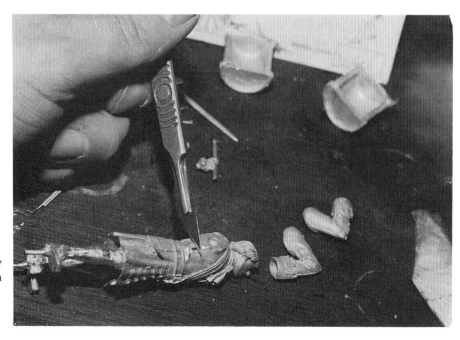

Locate and remove the raised lines left by both halves of the mould. They can be scraped away with a scalpel blade and then finished off with a needle file.

Using a wire suede brush to clean up the castings; in this instance it's the round base that is receiving attention. All parts should be cleaned until they are bright. *Bottom left*: the flux used for soldering white metal is liquid and applied with a brush. It has a mild acid base and is water soluble, so it must be washed off with clean water when all soldering is complete.

joints works well if the flux has been applied sparingly. However, support of the parts is necessary because the solder takes a few seconds to solidify. Remember, iron and solder must be applied simultaneously to the fluxed joint for the best results.

Securing figures to white metal bases, as supplied with some figures, is very easily carried out by this method. By working from underneath the base the spigots on the bottom of the figure's feet can be 'invisibly' secured, allowing no solder to come between the soles of the figure's feet and the base.

Arms, heads and such extremities cannot normally be soldered directly, but they can be sweated into place. Clean and flux both jointing surfaces, then give each a thin skim or film of solder. Locate the part and support it – in the case of an arm, wire to the body and compress the joint with a wire twist. Apply a clean soldering iron to the arm and observe the joint, watching for the solder to liquefy due to heat conduction and then transfer to the solder within the joint. The solder has a much lower melting

Left: with the work supported, the base is attached to the figure by first applying flux then bringing the iron and low-melt solder to the job simultaneously whenever possible. *Bottom left*: tinning the head and hat with solder. *Bottom right*: with the hat in place the iron is applied to the top of the hat and with heat induction the hat is secured as the solder liquefies.

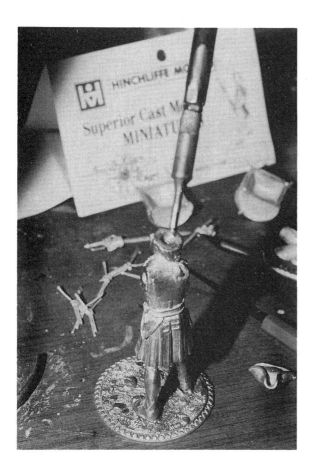

point than the metal the figure is made from, so no damage will be done to the surface of the casting where the iron is applied.

If possible, apply more pressure to the joint as the solder melts; if compressed a little more, as the solder melts it will exude from the joint. When the joint is made, any excess solder around it can be removed with a quick wipe with the iron; but do not apply any flux on the joint and do clean the iron's bit with flux first.

After soldering is completed, wash the figure in warm soapy water. Washing-up liquid is an excellent water-based flux remover and all residues must be removed

Top: with the work supported, preparations are made to solder the arms in place. The drum is attached to get the arms in the right configuration. *Left*: arm and body join are tinned then the arm sweated in place by applying the iron directly to it. Low-melt solder has good gap-filling properties.

The completed figure which should now be washed in water containing a mild detergent to remove flux and solder residue.

from the surface. Next check for any gaps or surface pitting which can be filled or 'stopped' with more solder, then give the figure a final wash, immersing it completely in soapy water. A good scrub with an old toothbrush does not go amiss either.

Before priming give the figure a final check – you're bound to have missed something and it would be very difficult to correct when you're half-way through painting the figure. If you have used glues, epoxy or cyano, check especially the arm, head and leg joints if the kit is multi-part.

Priming

Priming white metal figures before paint-

ing is necessary for the paint to adhere to the castings and it should always be done carefully. It not only shows up any imperfections missed in the other preparatory stages but provides a good undercoat for any colours used. White metal, untreated, is a very poor medium on which to paint, especially if you wish to use oil paints.

Before priming, the castings should be spotless; don't hesitate to wash the figurine as much as possible as the paint will adhere all the better for it. Always ensure that you rinse thoroughly in cold, clean running water straight from the tap. Some modellers don't even wash the casting once from taking it out of the box, gluing it together and then painting it. Then they wonder why the paint won't stick and in a short time wears off or even, in some cases, flakes away. There are, of course, those who will tell you that washing the casting is all baloney and that it is not necessary. The choice is yours.

Priming can be sprayed or brushed on. The former application is preferable because it ensures (if done correctly) that a fine coat is evenly distributed all over the figure. Brush application if done carefully, however, works well and should not be looked upon as inferior.

Choice of the primer colour is personal and one that will be adopted with experience. Clear varnish, matt white enamel or light grey enamel are all used, as are the basic colours – in enamels or acrylics – that the figure will, ultimately, be painted in. For a figure with a red tunic and blue trousers, for instance, matt red and blue enamels are painted on directly over the white metal. This ploy is used by some modellers who paint exclusively in oils.

If metallic enamels are to be used, undercoat black or dark blue for iron, yellow for brass and bronze and white or very light blue for silver. Again, experimentation is advised.

Matt white auto-primer spray is an

Figures undercoated with matt white acrylic paint. The paint was applied with an airbrush. These are Le Cimier 54mm figurines of Major General Dorsenne (left) and Major Kirmann of the Mamelukes.

excellent undercoat and primer for white metal figures. It is cellulose-based, but this does not matter on metal surfaces. Any paint can be applied over the top of it and it is durable, drying to a perfect matt finish with a very fine grain, favoured by some modellers as a good key for paints. Auto-primer paints can be found in any shop dealing with motor spares.

Matt white enamel sprays are ideal too but, if the can is not shaken properly or for long enough to thoroughly mix the paint, a less-than-satisfactory finish results. Most aerosols include internal 'agitators' which should be rattled for a good five minutes or so before spraying. You simply do not know how long the can has been standing on the shelf before you bought it.

A point to remember when spraying with aerosols, or any spray equipment for that matter, is not to make one heavy application in one pass of the can. Several thin coats 'misted' onto the model figure works far better than one heavy coat and gives a much more satisfactory finish. Remember, too, always spray in a well-ventilated area and, when finished, always cover the figure to stop dust particles settling on the drying surface. Keep the can at a respectable distance from the model figure too and, if possible, wear a disposable mask during all spraying sessions.

Brush priming is probably the most common method used for undercoating miniature figurines, and thinned white enamel is the most common undercoat

A 90mm scale Poste Militaire figure being painted (minus the head!) with its base drilled and screwed to a wooden block for ease of handling.

surgical gloves available which should alleviate any marking from skin contact. Make final checks for surface imperfections and, using a clean tissue to handle the figure, mount it on a handle so it can be manipulated during the painting stages. It must be secured so that it will not part company with the holder when held at various angles from the horizontal to the vertical. For smaller scale figures, a piece of large-diameter wooden dowel, such as a section cut from a broom handle, with a small square of wood screwed to one end, will suffice to mount the figure on. The figure can, if it is not complex and thus very heavy, be secured to this with Blu

The feet on this New Hope Design figure have been drilled to accept paper clip wire, which is either glued or soldered in place. The wires are then inserted into pre-drilled holes in a wooden block for support during painting.

used. As with spraying, apply thin coats, ensuring 'pockets' of dried paint do not form in the creases and other such areas on the figure. Use at least a No.5 brush and do not overload the bristles with paint before use. Always allow primer coats to dry for at least 24 hours before painting, otherwise you could find, if you're impatient to get going, that the paint you use could 'lift' the undercoat.

After you've primed a figure, do not handle or finger its surface again because of the natural oils present on your skin which will impair the painted surface. If you must handle the figure, there are thin

Tack or self-adhesive pads available in stationers. However, plastic figures can be adequately secured in this manner but metal figures, especially larger scale types, may need other more substantial methods.

Where the mass of metal dictates a really secure mounting, alternative methods are needed. If the figure has a cast base in the kit, secure this by drilling a hole in it (don't worry – it can be filled later) and putting a woodscrew directly through it into a wooden handle. Do not position the screw hole so that the figure, or parts of it, will be over the screw or removal later on may be a problem. Also ensure that the holes in the base to take the spigots of the figure's feet do not foul the handle.

Where no cast metal base is supplied, or spigots are absent from the feet, holes must be drilled up into the feet and brass rod spigots or threaded bolts inserted and secured with glue or solder. These can then be inserted in pre-drilled holes in a block of wood or similar.

Drill the holes for a short way into the bottom of the feet, into the heels, and thus into the mass of metal constituting the legs. This will give a more secure support and be less likely to come adrift during painting, which would be a disaster.

Alternatively, use a self-tapping screw or bolt to secure the figure to a plywood or thick plastic plate via the drilled hole. Then secure the plate to a handle ready for maximum support during painting.

Whatever the method used, the figure must be absolutely secure for painting. It's almost impossible to hold a figure by its extremities while you paint it. Besides, it defeats the object of cleanliness and the results of handling from skin contact being transmitted to the model which would otherwise destroy the smooth clean primer surface. Take time over your preparations and don't rush them.

Mounted figures can be supported by drilling into the buttocks, inserting a piece of wire or rod and then insert this into a pre-drilled hole in a block of wood.

I have touched on converting metal figures, albeit briefly, and stated that it is a practice not many modellers, especially beginners, care for. A conversion can exist in many forms. Simple additions to a stock figure and a different paint job could be termed a conversion, and would certainly make it different from the stock castings made up and painted from the kit to the manufacturer's instructions. It is a challenge and fun, however, to cut and reposition arms and legs in a different posture, so altering the figure considerably. Also, interchanging of parts, even plastic and metal, works, so don't be afraid to mix your mediums at any stage of the game. All you have to do is ensure that everything is in proportion, because one manufacturer's concept of a common scale may not match that of another.

Some one-piece castings cannot really be converted, but characters can be changed by simply altering the position of the head, which, in fact does cause considerable change of any figure's posture. Just compare the stock casting with one where the attitude of the head has been altered, and this becomes clear.

Major conversions are not easy for beginners, who may look upon any mistakes as very expensive, and these are something that should be worked up to but, if you can convert plastic figures with complete success, metal should not prove difficult at all.

A fine piercing saw is a necessity and a soldering iron does make life much easier than glue and a lot of filler. Make sure all cuts in white metal are made cleanly and that the work is always well supported and securely clamped while you attend to it. It is something that requires practice and a logical step-by-step approach.

White metal figures can be 'carved' to a limited degree but it is much easier to remove metal – and replace it – with a soldering iron. Begin with simple conversion – such as interchanging parts, altering head, arm and leg positions – and graduate to completely different postures which should give you practice for scratchbuilding your own figures at some later date.

Find out which manufacturers have 'spares' in their ranges. This is no problem for plastic figure converters in 1:32 – 1:30 scales with the vast Historex range of spares . . . but Scale Link, Verlinden, Hornet, Puchala, to name but a few, all produce – mainly – spare heads, and other parts, for converters and scratchbuilders; bare heads and ones with various forms of headdress are available and these ranges are definitely worth investigation.

Larger scale modellers are not so well catered for as the 54mm figure modeller but, with a lot of searching, various spares including firearms and swords can be found. Once you've mastered human conversions, try horses – in metal they're a whole new 'ball game' when compared to the plastic types.

At the time of writing, Francois Verlinden has embarked on a wide range of spares for his 120mm scale resin range which enables many different figures to be produced. Clearly there are benefits from having a practising modeller run his own company – he knows what fellow modellers want and is providing it.

PAINTING

Painting a figure cannot really be taught from a book and, again, practice and experimentation are needed. Guidelines can be given, but ultimately it is down to the individual modeller and his or her dexterity with the paintbrush that counts in the end. However, some 'dos and don'ts' can be passed on (see colour sections).

If you know someone who can paint figures, the obvious course is to sit down with him – if he's willing of course – and be shown how to paint, step-by-step from square one. Joining a local modelling club with military modelling as an exclusive interest should produce such a tutor.

Copy other modellers' styles and how they do it. Use the same mixes of colour and, if need be, slavishly copy them until you become competent and proficient in the art and no longer need any guidance. When you are competent and satisfied with your results, then deviate from the pattern you've become accustomed to following and develop your own style. This you must do, otherwise you will simply be a clone of your instructor.

The face of a model figure is all-important – it's usually the first thing that captures the viewer's attention. An excellently painted face can 'lift' an otherwise mediocre figure, whereas a not-so-good face can make an excellent figure mediocre. Realism is transmitted from a lifelike miniature face whereas a carelessly painted face simply destroys any illusion of realism. Not everyone is good with the brush, however, and in the end it is only practice and yet more practice that brings rewards.

At first, keep your colour mixes simple and do not opt for many of the published 'multi-colour mixes' to obtain a flesh colour. Remember also that your painting must represent the figure as a human would appear from a distance. Begin about 15 yards (13 metres) or so away with a friend as the 'model'. Ask him or her to approach you, and notice how the facial details alter from obscure to distinct as your subject nears you. Then try it with you holding a figure at arm's length and the subject approaching to match that height in your direct forward vision. What you see on the human subject should form a rough guide to what you're trying to achieve on the miniature figurine's face. So many people forget this and 'overpaint' the face to distraction. The heavy lines and shading produce something resembling a 'frog prince' which bears little resemblance to any human features. Turning what should be normal into something ugly is a trap that is easily fallen into. Although figures should be painted in similar style to an actor putting on stage make-up, they should not be overpainted to the point where they resemble a circus clown.

Eyes are very important. Never paint them black! Never paint eyeballs white and never show the eyeball completely, unless the figure is to be depicted in the act of some wide-eyed action pose. White for the eyeballs should have the merest touch of light blue – and the eyeballs are brown, blue or green, or shades thereof, not black which is too severe a colour and will completely unbalance an otherwise correctly coloured face.

Painting in oils offers the added advantage of enabling unsuccessful attempts to be wiped away. With acrylics or enamels, wait until the paint dries then paint over it. Use a brush well suited to the task, one you're happy with, but not too big for faces.

The slow-drying properties of oil paints make them by far the most suitable medium for painting animal skins such as on this Poste Militaire figure of Attila the Hun.

An 00 is a good one to start with when you're getting the feel of painting faces.

A very basic flesh tint for European skins is mixed from Yellow Ochre and Titanium White with a minute spot of red for fresh complexions. Darken this mixture with a brown tint such as Burnt Umber, in varying degrees, and use it as a shading tint. Highlight the mixture by adding more Titanium White. Therefore, your basic palette for flesh should have three pre-mixed shades before you begin. Follow the step-by-step photos to see how a figure's face is painted with oils.

Painting the uniform and clothing is next. Before you start, you must ascertain from which direction the light comes and where the shadows and highlights will fall on the figure. As with flesh tones, darken or lighten the basic shades and apply shadows and highlights accordingly. Do not overdo this procedure, and ensure that the colours blend and do not end in hard demarcation lines as they graduate from shadow to highlight. Once mastered the technique will become easier and virtually second nature. Brush out the paints thoroughly and do not overload the brush. The object is to spread the paint evenly and not to layer it on in thick coats. Blend with a dry brush on large areas such as clothing where light and shade must not be overpainted.

Representing dissimilar materials, such as fur, leather and metals, requires different treatments. This is especially so if a convincing metal effect is to be achieved on plastic. As most clothing is matt in appearance, leather produces a contrast in that its surface is shiny. Fur also has highlights which it needs in the painting stage to emphasise depth.

'Metals' need an undercoat and finishing coat to seal the grainy surface they leave when dry. Enamel metallic paint should not be mixed in the tin, but the sediment scooped from the bottom, deposited on a palette and thinned to the required consistency with the solvent in which the paint is bound. It is then applied to the model, brushing out smoothly as you progress, but trying also to avoid overpainting. Use two thin coats instead of one thick one.

An innovation in metallic colour paint is Humbrol's 'Metalcote', which contains metal particles. The paint is applied by brush – preferably sprayed on by airbrush – then allowed to dry for about 30 minutes and buffed to a highly polished finish.

Lace on the figure's coat tails must be treated differently to that on the guard of the sword hilt. Do not use neat metallic paints for uniform lace.

Practice and experiment with these colours has shown that, once again, two thin coats are better than one thick one. Unlike conventional metallic paints, and because they have metal particles added, 'Metalcote' colours should be stirred thoroughly. The sediment alone can be a little too thick and will not disperse correctly unless thinned a little at a time to obtain correct consistency.

As mentioned, ordinary metallics can dry to a grainy finish and benefit from a coat of acrylic varnish – the clear variety – to produce a smooth finish more like a real metal surface. Ensure that the paint has dried out completely before painting varnish over the top, as varnish has a habit of lifting uncured paint very easily.

Where metallic lace is found on uniforms, do not paint it in metal colours. Nothing looks worse, or more gaudy or unreal. Use paint, Yellow Ochre for gold, greyish blue for silver, highlighted and shaded to represent the lace. Experiment by adding a little gold powder which introduces minute highlights to the lace, but don't overdo it, and practice off the figure first.

Try all different types of paint for your figures and mix them together too. Experiment as much as possible to achieve different effects and try mixing enamels with oil paints and also the different water-based types together. Try adding gesso powders and talcum powder to paint to see what textured effects you can achieve.

Horses are not easy to paint convincingly, especially when a beginner compares his first efforts with those of an experienced painter; it's enough to put anyone off! (see colour sections).

A simple, yet very effective, method of obtaining a good finish on horses can be made with a piece of sponge and oil paint. After assembly and priming the complete body, paint it in oils of the darkest shade. Next, a dry piece of plastic microcellular type 'sponge' is lightly rubbed over the surface, leaving the dark paint in all engraved detail and areas the sponge could not reach.

A highlighting colour on another piece of sponge is then applied with a dabbing motion over the area where the paint was removed with the first wipe. This forms the basis of an overall finish and leaves only the eyes, hooves and any markings to be put on with the paintbrush.

With horses, always try to refer to a real subject whenever possible. Different colours and types of horse have different coloured

muzzles, hooves and suchlike. If you have access to horses in a local stable where they can be seen without tack, take your camera loaded with colour film to take pictures of as many different coloured horses as possible to be used as painting references. Once you have a small 'library' of horse photographs, you should experience no problems in representing true colouring. Study the horse and how it moves too and, if you can, buy a reasonably good book on horses that will answer all your questions.

SCRATCHBUILDING FIGURES

Ultimately, many modellers will attempt to build a figure completely from scratch after using different commercial spare parts in complicated and advanced conversions.

Using Milliput for the first time also inspires many modellers. This useful medium, formed over an armature, is one of the most popular methods of producing a figure from scratch. It's also the easiest, especialy for small-scale figures.

The armature can be made up from soft wire – paper clips are ideal for small-scale figures – a loop for the head, single strands for the body, arms and legs with perhaps some thickening in the trunk areas. The armature must be in correct human proportions otherwise something unhuman will result! Milliput mixed up in small quantities should be added in small balls or pellets until the body shape is built up.

The head deserves, and must get, prime attention. It's not really worth continuing with the rest of the model unless you have a good representation of the human head to begin with. If you feel it is beyond your capabilities to sculpt a head, use one from a commercial spares range or take one from a figure in the scale you're in and adapt that. It's not 'cheating' – it's one of

Three stages of a Chota Sahib production figure, left to right: the master, a pre-production casting and the final production casting.

the prime requirements of spares ranges. Spare heads are not expensive, and do meet the modellers' immediate needs. In 54mm scale, of course, a good selection is available. However, the use of commercial parts does negate somewhat the description 'scratchbuilt'.

For building up figures, an alternative to the armature method is a 'dolly' which is the rough human shape, a sort of 'tubular skeleton'. From this can be cast, in RTV silicone rubber moulds, in white metal, as many 'dollies' as required. The metal castings will be thin enough to bend and animate before building up with Milliput, or whatever, to the required form. Once the ideal size is made and available as a casting, building up the rest in Milliput enables a collection of scratchbuilt figures, perhaps for a multi-figure diorama, to be built up fairly quickly.

CHAPTER 5
MODELLING MILITARY VEHICLES

Modelling armoured fighting vehicles (AFVs) is a popular facet of the military modelling hobby. Once lavishly catered to by an obliging plastic kit industry, the supply of new releases has now slowed down to a trickle. Other areas have captured the attention of the toy industry – yes, toy industry, because, make no mistake about it, plastic kits of miniature military vehicles are a product of this industry. They have to be, for the capital needed for investment in injection-moulded kits is considerable, and toymakers follow trends. The recent Gulf war saw an increase in interest, and sales, in Britain in Challenger tanks and Tornado aircraft!

The manufacture of plastic model vehicle kits centres around Japan, with a lot of the moulds being made in Korea where it's cheaper. Manufacturers are rotating some kit moulds and arranging tie-ins so that kits appear under more than one name.

Vehicle kits to 1:72 and 1:35 scales have been standardised by the Japanese and Italians, although there are some larger and oddball scales. The British company, Airfix (now part of the Humbrol concern) flirted with the idea of military vehicle kits some years ago and decided to swim against the rest of the world by adopting the traditional model soldier scale of 1:32 for its models. Airfix were supported by Monogram in the United States whose output of 1:32 scale models was greater than Airfix's. Both companies produced excellent kits, although their output was nowhere near as prolific as the Japanese.

Heller, the French plastic kit manufacturer, entered the field with some 1:35 scale models, mainly of, perhaps understandably, French vehicles. These were withdrawn from the market some time ago, but have been made available from time to time by Humbrol who acquired the rights.

Small-scale vehicle modelling has

A popular model of a self-propelled gun of WWII vintage from the Italian manufacturer Italeri. This is an injection moulded plastic kit to 1:35 scale.

always enjoyed a fairly large following in the United Kingdom where the scale of 1:76 has proved to be the most popular, despite the Japanese and Italian production of 1:72 scale model vehicle kits. Based on the Airfix introduction of 1:76 scale plastic kits of AFVs in the early 1960s, where modellers adapted and converted what was available, this aspect of the hobby has expanded and secured a devoted following which, at the time of writing, now appears to be on the wane.

Airfix based the scale of 1:76 on the so-called 'model railway scale' of 4mm = 1 foot or, as the kits were labelled, OO/HO, a confusion of scales because the British manufacturers had built the bodies of the locomotives to 4mm = 1 foot but adopted the Continental track gauge of 16.5mm (4ft 8½in) based on 3.5 = 1 foot or half O Gauge (7mm = 1ft). (See Chapter 1.)

Surprisingly a similar 'scale clash' was repeated by the Japanese Tamiya company with their early Sherman tanks, where the lower hull and running gear scaled out nearer to 1:32 scale and the upperworks were near to 1:35 scale. The box said 1:35 scale, but modellers' scale rules said otherwise. The 1:32 scale running gear did, however, come in useful for the many convertors and scratchbuilders in that scale!

It does seem that 1:35 scale is the one modellers have settled for simply because there are more kits available to choose from.

Limited production vehicle kits, to 1:76 and 1:35 scales in polyurethane resin, cannot match the cost per unit of injection-moulded kits, but modellers will pay for something they want – they always have and always will – and thus the smaller

An Italeri 1:35 scale model of the US M24 Chaffee built straight from the box. This injection moulded plastic kit shows the detail possible with this process before painting has taken place.

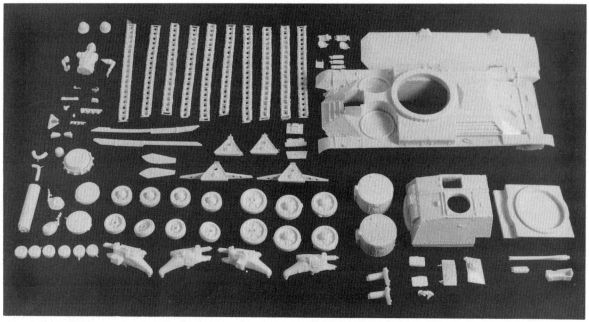

The many components of a polyurethane resin kit, which because of a labour intensive process in their production, tend to be much more expensive than an injection moulded plastic type. This is Cromwell Models' 1:35 scale British A9 cruiser tank.

manufacturers are receiving encouraging responses from their modelling clientele. The reaction to resin manufacturers 'filling the gap' has caused ripples in plastic kit manufacturing circles, where a steady trickle of new and re-issued kits have begun to appear at the time of writing.

Injection-Moulded Kits

Plastic injection-moulded kits far outweigh models produced in any other medium. They are mass-produced, and worldwide distribution facilities are available to the kit makers.

The amount of detail that can be incorporated into a plastic kit is phenomenal. Large-scale patterns, or master models, are made which are then reduced to the required scale by a pantograph system which reproduces the parts in solid steel blocks which form the (normally) two halves of the injection mould. Molten plastic under pressure is forced into the mould to produce the parts to make up the plastic construction kit.

Resin-Moulded kits

Largely devoted to much smaller production figures, the resin kit manufacturers fill a very considerable gap in the market and produce kits for AFV modellers who feel they cannot aspire to scratchbuilding.

The kits are produced from same-size masters, where the skills of the pattern-maker decide on the amount of detail incorporated in the kit. Resin kits have become sophisticated, equalling, in many cases overtaking, their injection-moulded counterparts in their attention to detail.

Kits can be very complex, or simple, and usually consist of around six parts in the smaller scales. In the case of a tank, this would be the hull, two-track units (moulded 'solid' with the wheels, sprockets, etc., *in situ*) the turret and gun. There may also be some smaller fittings such as exhaust silencer, anti-aircraft machine-gun or even a commander figure.

Larger 1:35 scale models now have many parts, including etched metal parts. Some even surpass injection-moulded kits for complexity.

Above: a combination of polyurethane resin and white metal components make up this Sovereign Models 1:35 scale Humber armoured car. *Below*: 'all-resin' Accurate Armour's 1:35 scale British Challenger of WWII.

Polyurethane resin has virtually super-seded polyester resin in model vehicle kit manufacture. It gives a much better definition in the mould and is easier to mix and pour, having a finer consistency, and it is less prone to the masses of air bubbles that seem to dog polyester resins during casting. Bubbles do occur in polyurethane resin, but these can be virtually eradicated with 'de-gassing' equipment which produces a vacuum expelling all air.

Polyurethane is not as brittle as polyester and can be assembled with general purpose glues. Cyanoacrylates are especially effective with it. It is far superior in many ways, not least in its ability to form finely detailed parts which would be impossible to mould with polyester.

Vacuum-formed Plastic Kits

Really available from only one major producer, Airmodel of Germany, vacuum-formed kits have not really been popular, perhaps because they need so much work doing to them to bring them up to acceptable standards. Once the assembly sequence is seen, many modellers would rather attempt scratchbuilding anyway.

Vacuum-formed models are not easy to build, and beginners are advised to stay away from the temptation of a comprehensive availability list until they are quite competent at assembling and converting injection-moulded plastic kits.

Metal Kits

One or two-piece small-scale white metal military vehicle models have been produced but, because of cost and weight, no doubt, they have been confined to mainly 1:76 scale – but there are exceptions!

Normally produced in a centrifugal castings machine, the same type model soldiers are cast in, white metal model vehicle kits are usually on a par with resin in price. White metal railway locomotive kits have been available for some time, and the majority suffer from the same faults – bad mould-making producing ill-fitting and distorted castings which have proved difficult to fit together. However, with careful mould-making, military vehicle kit manufacturers produce models of a good standard.

Kit design in white metal is important because the final assembly has one major minus factor – weight! White metal is very

A white metal kit of a Dorchester armoured command vehicle. This 1:76 scale miniature was produced by Lead Sled Models.

Outstanding foot figure designs from recent years are; *top left*, 90mm scale Spanish Conquistador by Andrea Miniatures. The blue armour finish is obtained by thin coats of Tamiya Clear Blue acrylic paint on the polished white metal areas of the kit. *Top right*, Regimental Sergeant Major of the Scots Guards to 100mm scale and painted in acrylic. A Cheshire Volunteer figure designed by Alex Williams. *Bottom left*, Le Cimier's 54mm personality figure of Marshal Ney painted in oil colours. *Bottom right*, Mike Good's 'Attila the Hun' in 75mm scale from Poste Militaire. Attila is painted in a mixture of oil, enamel and acrylic colours!

Left, top and bottom, a larger 90mm scale figure from Le Cimier representing a *cavalier* of the French *Garde Republicain*. This figurine kit was designed by Charles Conrad, is painted in oil colours and has had the cast helmet crest replaced with one from brushed-out nylon thread.

British figures are at *right*. *Top* is a 75mm British soldier of the late 18th century from Clydecast and painted in acrylic colours. It's a figurine which can be painted up into virtually any 'hat' regiment of the period. *Bottom* is a musketeer from Barton Miniatures – it's 90mm scale and painted in oil colours. Once again with little modification and a different paint job it can represent most regiments of its period . . . how about the blue coats with yellow facings of Luttrell's Regiment, ancestors of the present day Green Howards?

Quite a mixed bag! *Top left* is Andrea Miniatures 'The Gunfighter', a charming 54mm scale vignette from the Spanish manufacturer. *Bottom left* is the 110mm scale head painted in oil colours, and much enlarged here, of 'Sailor' Malan, a Poste Militaire figure designed by Mike Good. *Middle bottom* is a 90mm Empress Dragoon designed by Mike French and painted in acrylic colours. Note the splendid touch of a cat under the stool.

Top right and above, Verlinden Productions' 120mm scale resin kit of a US army Stinger missile operator. The kit was painted in oil and enamel colours by Marcus Nicholls.

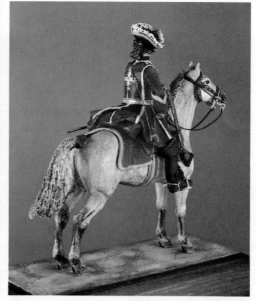

The 54mm scale figure shown on this page is neither a scratchbuilt or converted figure . . . it is built from an assortment of Historex spare parts. Historex kits are made up from polystyrene, injection moulded parts. The drawings at bottom were prepared for me by Eugene Leliepvre, the French military artist and, along with a colour print, formed the inspiration for the model. Horse and rider were painted in oil and acrylic colours.

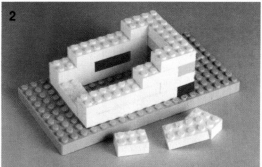

Casting parts with Room Temperature Vulcanising (RTV) silicone rubber and polyurethane resin is shown as a sequence on this page.

1. The master part – a 1:35 scale Sherman tank turret.

2. A mould box being assembled with plastic interlocking Lego pieces.

3. The master part in the box on a flat bed of Plasticine ready for the first pour of RTV rubber. The open hatch and gun apertures have been blocked with Plasticine.

4. The rubber, mixed to the manufacturer's instructions, has been poured up to the top of the mould wall. Always ensure a generous surround of rubber is made.

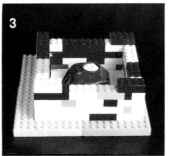

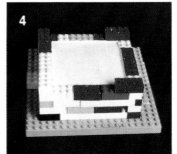

5. The mould with the first half, now inverted and still containing the master part, ready for the second pour. The mould walls have been removed for clarity in this photographic representation. The keys align the moulds during casting and have been cut into the rubber ready for the second pour.

6. The second half (blue rubber) has been poured into the mould. Again the front mould wall has been removed for clarity.

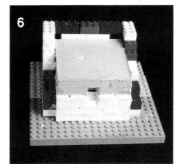

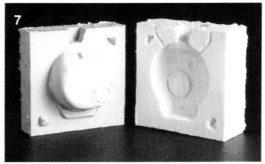

7. The finished RTV mould halves. The 'female' is white and the 'male' blue. Note the pouring and air vents have been cut into one mould face only.

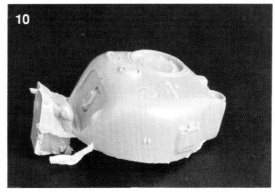

8. The mould supported by card walls and elastic bands (it must not be too tight which will distort the RTV rubber no matter how thick it is) with polyurethane resin being poured in.

9. A casting still located on the 'male' mould half shows how the resin has flowed into the pouring and two air vents cut into the 'female' half.

10. An unfettled polyurethane resin casting made from the mould with pouring and air vent plugs still in situ.

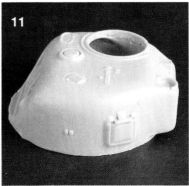

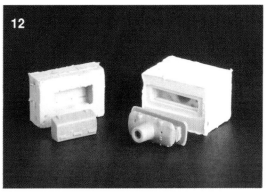

11. The finished part with the casting surplus of plugs removed. It's now ready for painting.

12. A gun mantlet and Sherman rear stowage bin cast from one-piece RTV moulds.

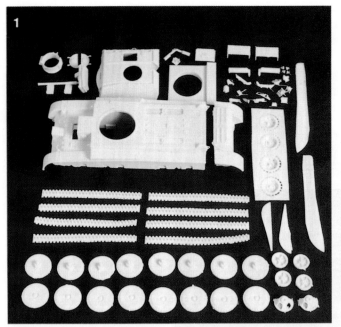

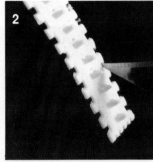

Polyurethane kits (sometimes with white metal and etched brass additions) are now becoming very popular. With care they result in excellent scale replicas.

1. The components of a kit . . . Cromwell Models' 1:35 scale British A13 Cruiser tank of Second World War vintage.

2. Flash is inherent in resin cast kits. Here the tracks are carefully cleaned with a scalpel blade.

3. Flash being removed from a wheel with the scalpel. Wheels must be true if the vehicle is to sit squarely on its tracks.

4. Removing the thin 'membrane' of flash in the turret aperture in the hull.

5. Cyanoacrylate or 'super glue' is the handiest adhesive to assemble resin vehicle kits.

6. The assembled A13 with the first coat of green paint applied.

7. After the second coat of darker green has been brush painted, the various markings are applied. Here the turret side wall receives 'C' Squadron's circle mark by a compass fitted with a bow pen loaded with thinned yellow acrylic paint.

8 and 9. The completed model with hand-painted markings for tank number T18102, appropriately named 'Cromwell' of HQ Squadron, the 3rd County of London Yeomanry, 22nd Armoured Brigade, 1st Armoured Division, United Kingdom. c.November 1940.

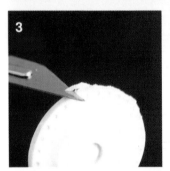

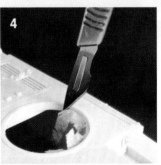

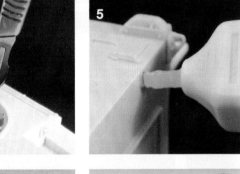

the British Humber Mark 1 armoured car designed by John Tassell and marketed under the Sovereign banner. *Bottom left*, Marcus Nicholls' Tamiya 1:35 scale uparmoured M2 Bradley (Operation Desert Storm) an injection moulded plastic construction kit redesigned to keep pace with modern trends. The model was built, painted and lightly weathered and a Verlinden Productions crew added. *Below*, Rolls-Royce armoured car of First World War vintage built from a Scale Link kit. The scale is 1:32 and the kit is made up of white metal castings and etched brass parts. Soldered construction was used throughout the assembly sequence.

An assortment of assembled and painted model vehicle kits. *Left* is Accurate Armour's 1:35 scale Soviet BMP1 cast in polyurethane resin. *Middle left*, one of the first 1:35 scale polyurethane resin and white metal kits of

Left, Bill Evans and David Parker's diorama posed against an outdoor backdrop of trees. The vehicle is the 1:35 scale Comet tank from Accurate Armour with white metal figures (stock and converted) from Hornet Models. (*Photo: Bill Evans.*)

Below, Marcus Nicholls' diorama of the Dragon Models 1:35 scale LSSC (Light Seal Support Craft) in a 'Delta' setting during the Vietnam War. The figures are by Verlinden Productions and Andrea Miniatures. The water was made from acrylic medium over a painted and varnished surface. The interesting Buddha statue is from the vast Verlinden range of kits and accessories. (*Photo: Manny Cefai.*)

An all white metal 1:32 scale kit of a World War One Lorry by Scale Link. The canvas tilts over the cab and body are represented by very thin lead foil. Kits such as this one lend themselves readily to soldered construction with low-melt solders and fluxes.

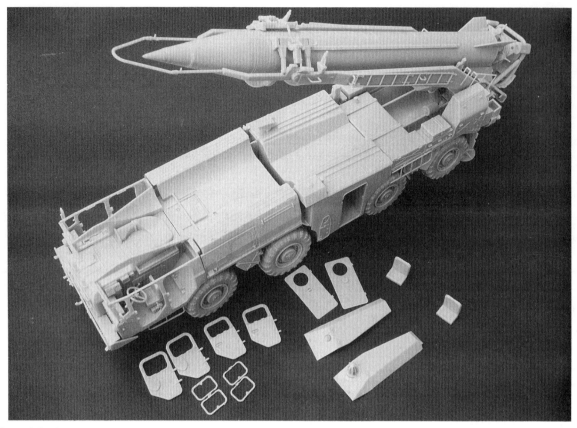

One of the largest 1:35 scale plastic kits of a military vehicle ever produced . . . the giant Soviet Scud B missile and launcher vehicle from Dragon Models, here under construction by Bill Evans.

A close up of Dragon's Scud B launcher shows interior detail included.

heavy and models made up in this material (especially butt-jointed, slab-sided pieces) are rather hefty and a little unwieldy when assembled.

There is a range of military vehicle kits cast in white metal made by the Scale Link Company (who also manufacture model railway accessories) to 1:32 scale and based on World War One subjects. The vehicles and guns are designed to be in scale with the company's comprehensive 1:32 scale range of World War One model soldiers and equipment.

Soldered construction is recommended for white metal kits: it not only produces a stronger model, but also enables any distorted parts to be bent into shape to fit. If one joint is secured previously, the part can be bent against a soldered joint, whereas with a glued joint this would not really be possible.

More kits are planned in white metal by Scale Link at the time of writing, possibly with the introduction of more etched metal parts to replace some of the white metal bits. It will be interesting to see more kits in etched brass, though, so far as I know, only one complete kit at present – a Renault FT17 by a French manufacturer – has been produced.

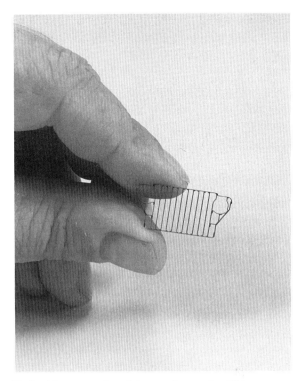

Etched brass to the ultimate degree by 'Show Modelling' of Japan . . . three parts were sandwiched together to obtain this grille for a 1:35 scale Jeep!

Photo-etched brass or nickel silver kits would, perhaps, be a boon to the military vehicle modeller, but it seems that, once again, the properties of this medium have been more fully developed by model railway kit makers. Some polyurethane kits have

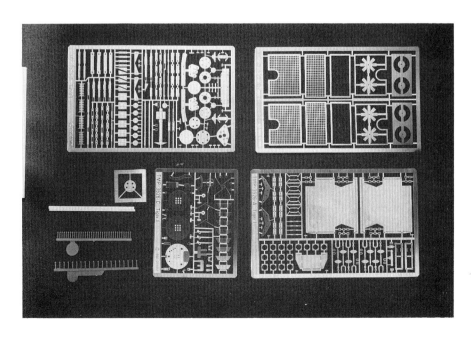

Etched brass and steel parts to detail a 1:35 scale plastic kit of the German Tiger I tank.

etched metal parts and Verlinden has produced many accessory kits for existing models.

BASIC KIT ASSEMBLY

Plastic vehicle kits, like soldier kits, need a fair amount of care and attention to achieve good results. Beginners can produce a fine model with their first attempt, but with a lot of tyro modellers the opposite is often the case.

The most important point is never to rush it! Take your time. It's fairly obvious we all want to see a collection of parts in a box transformed quickly into a work of art. While a model should not take a lifetime to construct, it should not be hurried to the point of ruin.

What follows are some pointers and advice for novices on plastic kit construction. It is difficult to generalise because individual model vehicles are nearly all different, but these tips are offered from quite a few years' kit building experience.

When you first open the kit box, do not remove any of the parts from their runners or sprues. Leave them in place and read the instruction sheets before you do anything else. It is difficult, granted, to keep your hands off the moulded detailed components, but you should only examine them after complete familiarisation with the instruction sheet.

Identify each 'group' of parts on its runner. Some manufacturers are good and group them logically, whereas others do not, which can result in an impractical layout. Next, check everything is there, Laborious, yes, but imagine getting halfway through building the model and you find that a part is missing. There's nothing more certain to make a modeller lose his temper than a missing part. It rarely happens today, but is not unknown.

Mould release agents are sometimes used and can be found on the surfaces of the kits parts, plus 'human grease' from handling, so it's advisable to wash everything, still on the runners, in warm soapy water. Household washing-up liquid is ideal for this. Soak the kit parts for about fifteen minutes then remove, rinse thoroughly with cold water and allow to dry out naturally. This process will ensure no grease deposits hinder the cement's action on the plastic during construction.

After washing, it's better to cut down the handling of kit parts to the absolute minimum and only when they're needed for assembly. When removing parts from the runners do not twist them until they are free, but cut them away with a sharp knife on a hard surface or with a pair of single edge cutters. Remove any mould part lines with a knife edge and fine abrasive. Polish up the part using 'Scotchbrite' or similar, for an extra special finish. This can't be used on very small parts, as they would probably become trapped within its open fibres but on large parts it's ideal.

Wherever possible, use liquid cement for construction and apply it sparingly. Remember that 'cement' is a solvent and it melts the plastic, so be very careful with it on small parts.

Follow the manufacturer's instructions for assembly, and only when you have a few models behind you should you adapt constructional methods to your own sequences. Also, as you progress, check the model against any published references. This is very important, and should be a mandatory part of your modelling. Any deviations can be corrected if they are of a minor nature during construction. Major mistakes will, more often than not, entail equally major corrective measures. Finally, give the model a final check and fill any gaps with body putty. Next, wash it again to get rid of any grease on the surface, which will probably inhibit paint adhesion.

Use a soft brush and wash the model, or alternatively soak the whole thing in warm water and mild detergent, rinse and allow to dry. This action will also get rid of any dust, plastic and natural. Avoid rubbing the plastic surface after washing because this will build up static and attract more dust particles.

PAINTING

Painting the model is one of the most enjoyable parts of the constructional sequence. This is just as well, as there is nothing worse than leaving an unpainted vehicle on display showing all the warts of the construction stages. This does not mean that the paintwork should cover a multitude of sins, including bad workmanship! Whether you use a brush or spray, the overall aim should be for a good even coverage without runs or imperfections.

Brush painting will be the course taken by most modellers and the first point with vehicle modelling is to use a brush to suit the size of the model. You will not get good paint coverage on a 1:35 scale vehicle with an 00 size brush, just as using a No.6 on a 1:76 scale tankette would be overdoing things somewhat. As with figure modelling, use the best quality of brush you can afford; sables are best, and just because the model is a tank it doesn't mean the work has to be 'slap-dash'. Cheap brushes do not last and they always seem to shed hairs where and when you don't want them to.

Mix the paint well, whether enamel or acrylic, and ensure that the consistency is correct. Decant the paint into a palette-type dish if you wish, but don't rush the task, and apply the paint in a succession of thin coats rather than one thick one. This statement is repeated throughout the book, but try it once and you'll really notice the difference.

Keep the brush strokes even and draw the brush in one direction only, allowing the paint to cover evenly. Do not brush over areas you have just painted and

Assembled and painted 1:35 scale polyurethane resin kit. This is Accurate Armour's Soviet BTR-60.

always allow paint to dry out thoroughly before overpainting. Avoid using small brushes on large areas which will only leave plenty of brush marks and not give a suitable maximum coverage.

Two or multi-tone camouflage patterns should be within the talents of most modellers. However, those that are sprayed on, such as modern United States army and Germany WWII schemes, are best done with an airbrush if they are to be convincing. So, at first stick to single colour finishes or multi-coloured patterns which are brush-applied on the real vehicle.

No comment will be made here on what are the 'correct' colours to paint military vehicles. Far too much time and energy and lots of hot air have been expended on trying to prove how 'correct' a colour is. Ask any serviceman, past or present, about a particular vehicle or equipment's colour and you'll probably get the same answer – they were all different! Time and weather alters colours and the limits of the human eye's colour perception, effects of light and shade does not always mean that colour is interpreted correctly. If you choose a colour, rely on the manufacturer's mix – it will be near enough, or near as anyone needs.

Spray Painting

Spraying, especially by airbrush and when done correctly, does produce a superior finish to that of the conventional paintbrush, and even more so on larger scale models. Larger scale models can be painted with the many aerosol-canned paints available. The major paint makers offer these in all the popular military colours, so it's possible to obtain the ones you need fairly easily. Aerosol cans, however, have their limits, but you may find using them with a cheap airbrush to paint your models produces a superior result to the paintbrush, and fairly easy to

Tamiya's 1:35 scale M2 Bradley with the first camouflage colour sprayed on.

Above: the Badger 100GXF airbrush was used to finish this Tamiya M2 Bradley. *Below*: a spray booth with fan extractor and filters will rid the modelling area of virtually all paint spray mist providing the work to be sprayed is directly in front of it.

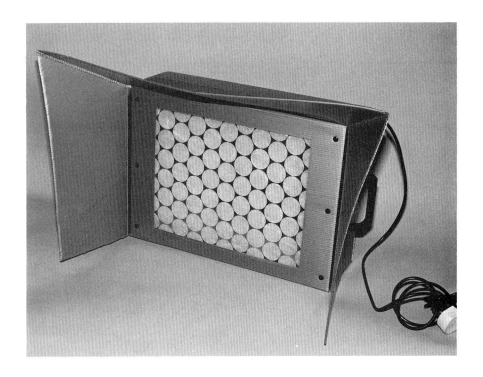

use. Always use a face mask when spraying with airbrushes or aerosols to inhibit the inhalation of spray mists – whether they be solvent or water-based, they will do no good to your respiratory system.

The model's surfaces to be sprayed must be scrupulously clean and the spraying done in a well-ventilated area. This does not necessarily mean out of doors because even the slightest breeze will deflect the spray's mist from its intended path. Also, ensure that any overspray does not, or cannot, settle on nearby areas. A large cardboard box with one side cut away is a good extemporised spray booth and, if you wish to buy the real thing, 3M do a version in expanded polystyrene. Graphic Air Systems produce an Aircleaner and Spraytrap which is a box containing an electric fan to suck spray mist into an internal filter. The box is supplied with a shroud and can get rid of a lot of airborne mist caused by spraying with the airbrush. The unit folds into a convenient case for carrying, but can be set up as a permanent spray station.

When spraying with aerosols you have little or no control over pressure, so keep the can at least a foot away from the model, further if possible. Do not be impatient, but cover the subject in several light coats. Do not begin spraying directly at the model but aim to one side then press the button and move across the model, from side to side, only releasing the button when you've passed the model completely. The spray must be kept parallel in its movement to the model's surface. Do not, under any circumstances, spray at an angle or haphazardly with aerosol can sprays, or attempt to 'spot' spray any areas with a direct burst onto the model's surface. This will result in thick blobs of paint in one area.

During spraying, try wherever possible to mount the model on some form of base that can be moved easily to enable all areas to be sprayed. A block of wood is suitable so long as it's big enough not to topple over, and can be reached easily to turn the model round during spraying.

Aerosol paint sprays are only good enough for covering the model with one colour, unless, of course, a hard-edged camouflage pattern is needed. Then only

A turntable lessens the handling of models when spray painting with an airbrush. This robust device is made by Southford Products.

by masking off areas of the base colour with masking film can the second colour be sprayed on.

Try experimenting with different-sized holes cut in a piece of card and held in front of the aerosol spray to reduce the area coverage. Good results and fair representations of sprayed mottled camouflage effects can be made by this method, but it needs care, attention, and practice to make it work properly without a lot of paint spatter.

Airbrushes

The airbrush is an expensive piece of equipment, but, once it's mastered, the modeller will wonder how he or she had managed without it in the first place.

Airbrushes need expertise in use and lots of practice is recommended for good results. However, there are cheaper types of airbrush available that are infinitely more flexible and better than aerosol spray paint cans. Although the simpler airbrushes are still powered by aerosols, they offer a finer spray and some degree of spray control.

Advice is usually given to begin with a cheaper, simpler instrument, and I have been guilty of offering these guidelines- . . . perhaps with economy in mind. On reflection, however, buy the best airbrush your pocket will stretch to, and also a compressor if possible. From the outset,

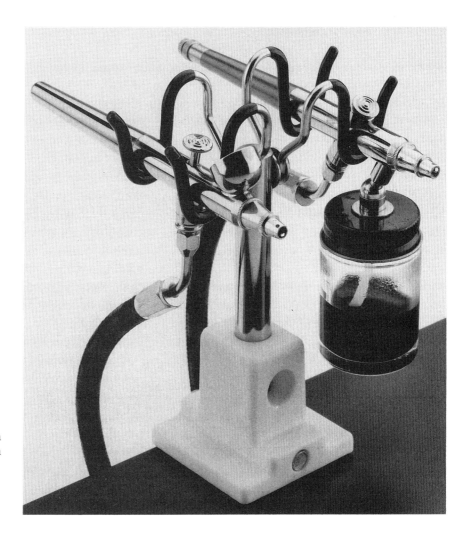

Two Badger airbrushes on a custom-made rest. Such a piece of equipment is essential to protect expensive equipment in use.

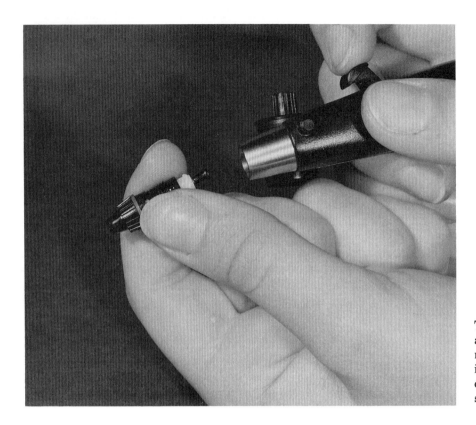

The revolutionary Aztek airbrush. The short needle is in the nozzle and is very easy to clean or change nozzles during a single spraying session.

practice makes perfect and, once you are adept at controlling the instrument, it seems silly to start with a simple airbrush that is very restrictive in its use only to change your operating procedures later and learn all over again.

Airbrushes come in different types, although they all produce the same basic result. Terms such as 'single' and 'double action' simply describe the method of paint and air control on the instrument. Double action brushes are controlled from one lever/button – press down for air and move the control back and forth for paint supply. This procedure is controlled by one finger. Single action types have a press down for simultaneous air and paint delivery. The actual amount of paint expelled is regulated by a movable nut acting on the airbrush's needle control.

A recent innovation is the Aztek airbrush. This has a different type of needle which is contained in the nozzle, and can be used as a single or double action airbrush. It has the normal lever control of the double action airbrush and also a knurled wheel on the body which can alter operation and spray patterns to the user's own choosing.

Outside and inside mix brushes are also available. The outside mix types are usually single action and the paint is supplied from an outside mounted reservoir and mixed with the air supply outside the instrument's body. Inside mix means just that; the air and paint are atomized inside the airbrush body and released via the nozzle.

More than ever before modellers are using airbrushes, and the results speak for themselves. This book is, however, for beginners and the purchase of an airbrush is not recommended at first, except for the really affluent, in the first stages of interest in the hobby, where other more important purchases are required. Graduate to the airbrush via conventional painting with a brush.

Verlinden Productions dry rub-down decals for 1:35 scale armoured vehicles. These are for modern Israeli and WWII Allied vehicles.

Decals or Transfers

Waterslide decals (or transfers as they used to be known) are usually a minimal part of any plastic vehicle kit, military vehicles not having a lot of 'decoration' such as is found on some aircraft.

Rub-down types of decal, exactly the same as dry lettering rub-down print, Letraset, Chartpak, etc., are not usually supplied, but they can be found in the lists of the many accessories manufacturers who advertise in model magazines. These decals are infinitely superior to the waterslide types, but more expensive.

Waterslide types are easy to use. Never soak them until saturated, but only wet them enough to release the decal from the backing. Apply them directly to the surface, position and blot dry, ensuring there are no air bubbles present. Where possible use a wetting agent which softens the decal enabling it to follow the contours of any uneven surface, such as rivets. Waterslide decals stick better to gloss surfaces, and do not go down well on matt paint finishes. An application of gloss varnish in the areas of the decal can be made, the transfer applied and, when dried out, oversprayed with matt varnish. Decal

carrier film is always glossy to some degree, even if the decals are listed as matt. Therefore, cut all decals out with a sharp scalpel blade and ensure you just skim the colour of the decal itself.

Weathering

Weathering is representing in miniature the effects of the elements on a painted surface. This can be loosely defined as fading, chipping and discoloration of paintwork; oil, grease and fuel stains with dust and mud splashes are also candidates. It must not be overdone, however, as nothing looks worse than badly done weathering! Applied in a haphazard manner nothing could be further from the fidelity to subject the modeller is trying to create. When weathering military vehicles, err on the side of light-handedness and try to represent, realistically, fair wear and tear.

One school of thought in vehicle painting favours a 'graduated' application of colour. Beginning with a base colour, successive coats are applied using the base colour to which is added a trace of white or a lighter tone. This shade is overpainted, but not overall, in the areas where depth is

Above: Cromwell Models' 1:35 scale A13 cruiser tank weathered with pastel chalks and powders. *Below*: similar treatment has been carried out on a 1:35 scale Trophy Models BRDM armoured car.

Trial matching of figures to vehicles for situations in dioramas. Russian and Afghan soldiers against a Soviet BRDM – a mixture of 1:35 scale vehicle and 54mm scale figures (54mm) which doesn't quite come off!

suggested by natural features, such as panel lines, raised angle irons, rivets, etc. This provides an 'artistically weathered' appearance on the model but it does need a lot of practice to be convincing. It can be done with both paintbrush and airbrush. Weathering will come with practice. Like painting model soldiers, it is difficult to describe, but easy to copy when demonstrated.

Powders are another useful medium. Use either powdered pastel chalks, obtained by rubbing the sticks on glasspaper to produce the powder, or powders sold for weathering models. The latter are finely ground powders with a slightly waxy texture which enables them to adhere to the model's surface. Carr's Modelling Products produce such powders in many different colours. Powders work especially well on vehicles intended for a desert environment, representing dust and sand, and can be brushed into upper surfaces to collect in a natural manner. Fix

pastels with a matt varnish spray to preserve the effect.

Dry Brushing

Dry brushing techniques are an important contribution to making weathered finishes. Dry brushing is easy, and best carried out with an old paintbrush – at least a No.5 size is best and the fluffier the bristles the better.

The brush is dipped in the paint only about 1mm – 2mm deep on the bristles and brushed to and fro over tissue to remove most of the paint. It is then lightly flicked over the model so that any raised detail receives a 'highlighting'. Again, do not overdo it, and keep everything low key. Do not, for instance, dry brush a model with white paint – it looks unreal and, frankly, awful. It is better to mix the base colour with white to obtain a highlight, and use that instead.

DISPLAY BASES

Whenever possible, make a base on which to mount your model. It need not be elaborate, but it should be neat and presentable with, perhaps, a nameplate with the vehicle's description. It is far easier to handle a baseplate than the model, especially if you've spent many hours on it. Dependent on the size of your model make sure that the base is not too big, but also ensure that no parts of the model, such as gun barrels, overhang it.

Attach the model to the base so that it will not move or, worse still, fall off when handled. The most secure method is not, as is universally thought and done, to glue the model directly to the base, but rather to secure it with a nut and bolt. Also, if you have included groundwork on your base make sure the vehicle 'sits' into it, especially if it's a tank. Remember, you're

representing an armoured, heavy vehicle in miniature so its tracks should not be shown perched on blades of grass!

The nut should be attached to the underside of the model. On tanks this is no problem and easily done during construction by drilling a hole in the hull bottom then gluing (use epoxy resin for strength) the nut inside the hull over the hole, so it can receive the bolt passed through a hole drilled in the base and up into the model.

If you put any terrain on the base, ensure that it is level, otherwise you will have to alter the position of the vehicle's suspension to follow the groundwork. This must be done early in the constructional stage, so think ahead.

The nut and bolt will still work with uneven groundwork, although the bolt hole may need to be drilled at an angle to locate and match up perfectly. Always ensure the bolt head is counter-sunk in the

Vac-u-Form units from Brian Sherriff make up a street scene base. The buildings have yet to be added.

A selection of wooden display bases for small dioramas and vehicles.

bottom of the base – for obvious reasons.

The base itself can be made up from laminate-faced chipboard with iron-on edging or, for a more attractive job, edged with picture framing or decorative beading, mitre-joined at the corners and glued and pinned in place.

Superdetailing

Once you have mastered kit construction, you will, no doubt, graduate to adding extra details. These may take the form of the vehicle crew's personal equipment or replacing solid moulded parts such as handrails with ones from wire or heat-stretched plastic. Any heavily moulded details look better if replaced with an in-scale part. Also, the parts that are the wrong shape, or have been left off due to their complexity, should be built up from scratch, and the model will be all the better for it. This procedure is known as 'superdetailing' and is the first step in converting plastic vehicle kits.

CONVERSIONS

Converting plastic vehicle kits, whether it is a minor or major conversion, is a satisfying exercise. Again, leave more ambitious conversions until later and begin with something easy, such as a turret replacement, or the up-gunning of a tank. This way, if your efforts don't come up to expectations you have not irrevocably destroyed any parts of the kit.

First, you will need a scale drawing or, alternatively, base the conversion on photographs if no drawing is available. You can produce your own drawings to scale for the parts which will make up the changes.

Conversions can be effected by cross-kitting; i.e. mixing of different parts of the same type of vehicle as made by different kit manufacturers. The US Sherman tank variants are a prime case where cross-kitting can produce different sub-marks of the basic vehicle. Often the mixing of parts from different makes of kit can be made to work very well, especially with World War Two types.

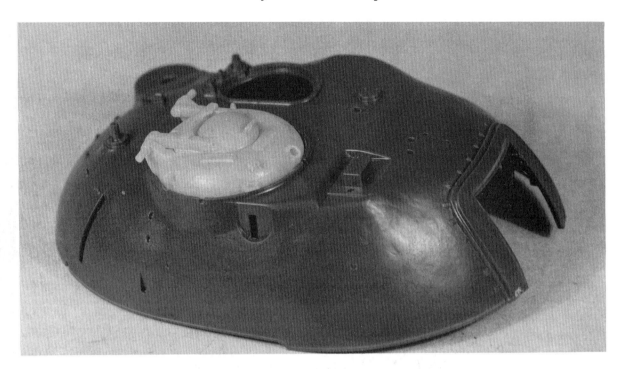

Small conversion parts and kits are popular amongst military vehicle modellers. Here an Israeli Urdan cupola moulded in polyurethane resin has been designed, like the real thing, to fit on plastic construction kits of US M60 and M48 main battle tanks.

With plastic card, a scale drawing and plenty of ingenuity, the conversion of commercial kits is a satisfying pursuit, as is the research and planning that go together to lay the basis of the actual alterations necessary.

SCRATCHBUILDING

It is difficult to define just where the dividing line between converted and scratchbuilt lies. With all scales, modellers tend to use available parts such as road wheels, tracks and 'standard' types of running gear parts. This is different from the true definition of every part being built entirely from scratch.

However, guided by competitions, it could be judged that if the complete body-work of a model was built from scratch using only the wheels and tracks on a tank – or the wheels alone on a truck or car – it could loosely be termed scratchbuilt. It certainly could not be called a conversion.

Hence the difficulty in drawing a definite line between the two.

Research is all-important. You should accrue as much information as possible. It cannot be said too often that you must exhaust every avenue of approach for information, both written and illustrative. Do not attempt a model on meagre information alone unless, of course, you are satisfied that no further information is available. Then, and only then, will you have to do some intelligent guesswork and make a start. Many times modellers have produced work from virtually nothing in the way of reference, only to find that 'someone' has been sitting on the material they have so sorely needed. Obviously, there is nothing than can be done in such a situation, but remember to smile if it happens to you, especially if some 'expert' pulls your model apart verbally – at a club meeting or in a competition. At least you learn from the experience!

Use the model press to have your requests printed for information. It usually costs nothing to have a 'please help' notice printed either in the news or letter columns,and usually does bring in very good results from helpful modellers.

Plastic card (polystyrene sheet) is a superb medium for scratchbuilding purposes, being easy to work and pleasant to use when compared with card and wood. Seemingly complex parts become an easy exercise using plastic card and quite difficult shapes are made easier by the very nature of the material. It is easily scored and snapped, which is preferable to cutting right through; it can be moulded fairly easily with home-produced plug moulds, heat-formed into circular structures; and, of course, it needs no special adhesives other than polystyrene cement, the liquid variety being by far the most suitable.

Scratchbuilders can vac-form it into quite complex shapes if they possess one of the rare Mattel vac-forming machines, now unfortunately taken off the market, but once a great help to modellers. Vac-forming can be done commercially by various companies, but you may have to place an order for a lot of parts. At the time of writing, there is no vac-forming machine suitable for modellers commercially available in the UK.

Commercial kit parts are also used extensively and copied by home-moulding techniques, which technically is an illegal practice. However, it would be very difficult to prove unless of course some 'enterprising' body began manufacture with the idea of selling the product. Court cases have arisen over plagiarism of model soldiers but none are known for anyone home-moulding commercial plastic kit parts for their own use. Some books and magazine articles even advocate the practice which appears to be, by convention, a widely accepted method of modelling.

Moulding rubbers are now widely available, and all military modellers should have a go at moulding their own bits and pieces. They are especially helpful to the military vehicle builder, in that he need only produce one master part to cast multitudes from – so handy when building the running gear of a tank, especially when you can't use or adapt any commercial parts.

A one kilo pack of silicone rubber moulding compound is a capacity ideal for modelling at home. The rubber is in the larger tin with the catalyst in the smaller. This Room Temperature Vulcanising rubber is now widely available.

The term RTV applied to moulding rubbers means that the rubber cures at room temperature (Room Temperature Vulcanising). A catalyst is added to the silicone rubber, mixed in and the rubber is poured into the mould and left to cure. Silicone rubber will mould the finest of detail and really must be tried by the modeller to ascertain its properties. Alec Tiranti produces a very useful little booklet telling all you need to know about making moulds from silicone rubbers and suitable casting materials. It is recommended that it be obtained and its methods put into practice. (See Appendix 1 for Alec Tiranti's address.)

Do not think that scratchbuilding a tank or truck is beyond your skills. Granted, your first finished scale model may not be your idea of the real subject in miniature. Its fidelity to prototype may be suspect but at least you will have 'made it yourself'.

Whatever the scale you choose to model in, try to stick to an easy subject first time round. You may find you're capable of a more complicated model, if so be guided by what you feel you can achieve within your skill range.

The majority of tank hulls are square structures, with lots of right-angled joints. Even today's advanced battle tanks are a basic box construction, despite any additional armours, panniers, add-on equipment and suchlike mounted over or attached to this basic shape. So, before you begin, ascertain those basic shapes of hull and turret and work out how you will achieve the shapes.

If you decide to model a vehicle where a scale drawing is available, take off the measurements for all parts that make up the hull, using all views and allowing for any angled pieces. If the drawing is a different scale from the one you normally work in, these measurements should be scaled up or down onto your own plan. Use graph paper for easy transfer and a pocket calculator to check your measurements. You should end up with a collection of drawings or templates of all the major components to the scale in which you're modelling. All that's left is to transfer these to plastic card.

Ensure that you allow for any plastic card thicknesses and which parts will butt joint over or inside others.

Assembly should be made on a completely flat surface. A piece of thick glass is ideal to set up all the cut-out parts on, and is also useful for cutting out on. Begin by fitting the hull sides to the floor and then all the parts, making up the engine deck front and rear armour plate. Use a square to ensure everything is correctly positioned and an adjustable square for any angles. On larger scale models, internal bracing or bulkheads may be necessary, so put these in at the preliminary stages. Also decide if you are to have an open turret ring on the hull top. If so, this should be cut out of the part with a compass cutter *before* the whole part is removed from the plastic sheet.

If the turret is made up from flat plates, it can be built up just as the hull was. If it is a cast type, two methods are possible. In small scales it can be carved from wood, sanded and finished, or shaped from laminated sheets of plastic card. For the larger scales, a wooden master can be carved and the turret plug moulded.

Plug moulding is where a master former is pushed through previously heated plastic card pinned securely to a piece of wood over a hole having the same outline shape as the master former. The master is plunged quickly and firmly through the hole, where the heated plastic card is formed around it. Shapes which curve in under the turret wall to the ring (undercuts) should be made as two-part formers. They can be bolted together for shaping for accuracy then parted and used as separate plug moulds. Turrets in 1:35 scale can be made this way.

If, at first, the plug does not go through the hole cleanly, reheat the plastic and try again. A domestic oven hotplate or grill is ideal for softening the card. Do not use a naked flame. Wear gloves to protect the hands from heat when plug-moulding.

Wherever possible, roadwheels should be used from kits or adapted, although it's not overly difficult to produce them from scratch yourself. Likewise, the trackwork can be used and adapted. If nothing is available, however, you'll have to scratch-build. Wheels can be built up from discs and 'washers' cut from plastic card with a compass cutter. The ideal method is to produce as near perfect a master as you can, then make a mould of the part in RTV silicone rubber, from which identical castings can be made. This goes for the idlers and sprockets and any return rollers too – make one pattern and cast many, as it would be tedious to make each wheel individually, considering the amount needed for the average armoured vehicle.

Trackwork is not too difficult to scratch-build. Simple plate tracks are no real problem, but skeleton-type tracks need a lot more expertise and lots of care, especially in the larger scales. A master can be made up from plastic card of about six links in length. Also, make one or two individual links which will be needed to form around the idler and sprocket wheels. Make a two-part mould which will enable the teeth to be included also. Cast the track in 'runs' and fit these to the model. Polyurethane resin is superb for moulding tank tracks.

The track master must have perfectly square ends when you make it, otherwise any castings produced will not lie straight over the roadwheels and will twist out of true when glued in place. Working tracks and suspensions are something else, and beyond the scope of this basic discussion on scratchbuilding scale military vehicles.

Trucks, cars and other softskin vehicles can be, in the majority of cases, a little more difficult to scratchbuild, especially if they have many compound curves, such as wings, bonnets, hoods and the like. This is especially so for civilian models adapted or pressed into military service. Vehicles built specifically for the military tend to

A polyurethane resin casting of a 1:35 scale T34 turret produced from a mould made by me from a master by Vasko Barbic.

have more angular lines and are much simpler shapes overall.

Again, kit parts, and especially wheels, are most useful, and the scratchbuilding of these items and casting copies off is recommended. Tyres are made in standard sizes, so a range of tyre masters could be made up as you progress, as can the wheels and hubs. Masters, using the compass cutter, can be made up from laminations of plastic card. The tread is another matter and needs thought. Fortunately, unlike the fine slots in civilian tyres, most military tyres have huge track-grip treads so it's not impossible to cut a passable representation of the tyre tread on your master. A two-piece RTV silicone mould will give many castings.

Rounded wings can be plug-moulded in plastic card from wooden formers or a pattern carved from the solid and then moulded up. The inside of the mould is then lined with thin wax and the other half of the mould poured to form a 'shell'. This takes experimentation and works well with polyurethane resins which pour easily without too much trouble into two-part moulds.

Cabs, bodies and suchlike are similar in construction to the basic 'squared' tank hulls, but a chassis will need care to ensure it is perfectly true. Chassis can be built up from Plastruct sections where the channel-shaped sections are readily available, especially for larger scales.

There is a lot more work in the average truck than many modellers expect, because much of it is visible – the supports between the chassis and body, fuel tanks, brake linkages, differential bell-housings, chassis cross-members and supports, and much more. Look at any truck and you will appreciate what needs doing.

Scratchbuilding is something all modellers should aspire to – it is, perhaps, the most rewarding part of military modelling.

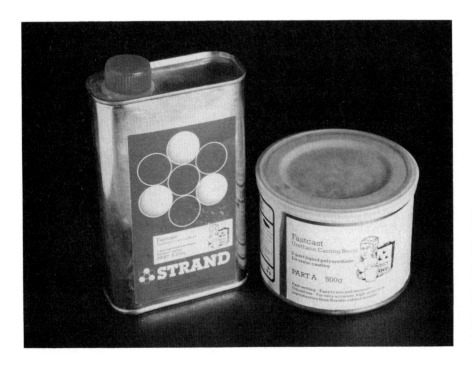

A one kilo modeller's pack of polyurethane resin as marketed by Strand. The resin is in the squat tin, the catalyst in the taller. Polyurethane resin is normally mixed 50–50 hence each container displaying a 500 gram legend.

CHAPTER 6
DIORAMAS

The word 'diorama' covers a broad canvas of modelling, from open-type miniature scenic settings on bases to ingeniously-lit boxed dioramas, or shadow boxes as they're also known. Another word associated with models in scenic settings is 'vignette'. This term is found in competition rules and usually means up to a maximum of three figures on a scenically-dressed base, though you won't find this description explained in any dictionary!

Dioramas fall into two categories – open and boxed. The former is viewable from any side, plane or angle, whereas the latter normally only allows the viewer to see what the builder wants him to from one viewpoint. It will come as no surprise

to discover that open dioramas are, therefore, more commonly encountered than boxed types. The latter do require a certain expertise and, more often than not, artificial lighting to create an atmosphere within.

At the time of writing, there is a book in print titled *How to Build Dioramas* by Sheperd Paine (see Appendix 3 for details), who is a master of the art. This book should be sought out, read and then read again. It is an absolute mine of information and, although it does not exclusively cover pure military dioramas, they do make up most of its content. It is written by an American for an American readership, and thus some of the terms and

Brian Sherriff's Vac-u-form sections made up into a country lane and stuck onto a base to form a crossroads. The tank is Accurate Armour's 1:35 scale Cromwell.

materials may be strange to readers in other countries. However, this does not lessen the book's appeal, with its excellent design and the knowledge and methods for diorama building passed on by the author.

Planning

Planning is an all-important consideration for the diorama builder. First, the most successful dioramas tell a story which needs only the minimum wordage on a descriptive label. Also, balance is very important in any diorama, open or boxed, as a base that is too large with figures congregating in the centre destroys all illusions.

A small overcrowded base will have the same effect. Therefore, planning means just that – a story line, good composition, correct base size centred on the model or models involved, scale ratio and, above all, good modelling completes the scene in miniature.

Boxed dioramas are governed by the same parameters, but internal manipulation and lighting must produce a good effect, so planning is even more important. It is wise to make a 'model of the model to be built' – in this case, a simple composition built up from cardboard will suffice – plus lots of sketches to enable the correct positions of the models to be established inside. As always, take plenty of time in the planning stage to map out exactly what you wish to convey.

Lighting

Boxed dioramas can show outdoor scenes but usually, because of their very direct and enclosed construction, depict interior scenes where all the lighting and shadow effects can be adjusted by the builder to the best advantage.

The outer box should contain the inner scene inside it, forming its own box with the interior angles arranged to convince the viewer's eye that what it sees is all perfectly composed and symmetrical. Walls, for instance, must be so shaped that perspective appears correct, even though it isn't due to foreshortening because of depth limitation. A lot of modellers employ different scales of figures to produce subtle perspective effects which help to cement the illusion firmly in the viewer's mind.

Lighting is not complicated, but is definitely experimental to the point of being set up by mainly trial and error. It can be supplied from an overhead low wattage strip light or from various angles via miniature bulbs powered by batteries or a transformer supply. Just as for set-ups for a real live stage show or play, the lighting must be adjusted until the effect is exactly what the modeller is seeking. No two dioramas will ever be exactly the same and each individual will require a different, often a wholly different, approach to illumination.

Fibre optics can play a great part in miniature illumination and effects and offer a reasonably-priced medium for experiment. Fibre optics are acrylic fibres of various diameters, from virtually a hair's breadth to about 2mm–3mm diameter, which will transmit light throughout their lengths from one single light source. Acrylic rods in the Plastruct ABS plastic range will work similarly for larger displays. The fibre optic works, because of its molecular structure, by transmitting light along its length. Place a light source at one end of a piece of fibre, which can then remain straight or be bent into any shape or direction, and that light source, whatever its colour, will appear at the other end of the fibre. By cutting the ends to different angles, different effects can be obtained.

Coloured lights are possible too by

TV Models of Scotland produce this plaster cast country road section for model vehicles. This one has scenic dressing added – a hedge from rubberised horsehair and static grass verges.

placing a coloured screen (coloured cellophane chocolate sweet wrapper works!) between the bulb and the end of the fibre. The muzzle flash of small arms or artillery caught at the moment of discharge, lights on vehicles and their instrument panels, candles, torches and fires, to list but a few effects, can be very realistically depicted with fibre optic.

Buy a pack and experiment yourself. Who knows, modellers are innovators – you may discover something nobody has thought of doing!

Earthwork

Top dressing for groundwork from natural materials is easy to collect, grade and prepare for use in diorama work. At the side of the road or driveway at your home a lot of 'dust' collects at the edges, thrown there by vehicles. This natural 'scatter' material is easily scooped up into a container and sifted through a cheap plastic tea-strainer which will eliminate a lot of the bigger bits, such as small pebbles inadvertently included. However, smaller

pebbles do have their uses, so don't throw them away; they can be used in certain model environments, such as where a lot of ground surface damage has been made by shelling, or earthworks dug and where small rocks will have been blown or shovelled to the surface.

Nothing looks more distracting than small natural pebbles 'balanced' on the groundwork or pushed into it with little surround ridges formed. Avoid this at all costs – the 'perching' of pebbles on the groundwork to represent rocks and their incorporation into the terrain really separates the 'absolute mess' from the model. If you model such terrain, mix the pebbles well into your groundwork foundation material, rather like currants into a cake mix!

Never, under any circumstances, leave natural terrain materials unpainted. They may look good off the diorama or in their own environment but, when the models are added, they take on an unreal appearance. It may appear a contradiction in terms to treat natural material with unnatural toning down procedures to look 'natural' but it must be done. The natural material forms the texture, not necessarily

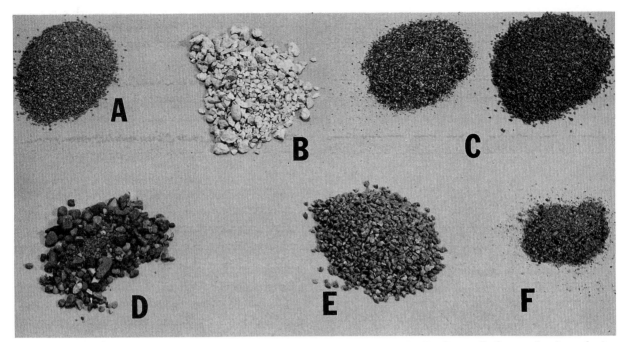

Readily available scenic base texture materials: A. Fine dyed sawdust. B. Cat litter. C. Coarse dyed sawdust. D. Grit from a seaside beach. E. Model railway track ballast. F. Fine dust from the roadside.

the colour. Paint and dry brush the surface texture just as you would any unnatural materials.

Materials for the actual groundwork and contouring are many and varied. For small areas epoxy putty, such as Milliput, is ideal, but its cost denies its use on any grand scale. Das Pronto self-hardening modelling clay, which needs no firing, can be sculptured very easily with simple modelling tools. Large areas are best covered with a plaster mix or Polyfilla in either powder or ready-mixed form. Tetrion is tougher and more textured and good for rock and stonework.

Before laying down fillers onto a solid diorama base score the base with a cross-hatched pattern to enable the groundwork material to adhere. Mix in some colour too, powder or water colour, and preferably a dark one such as a very deep brown, so that if any cracks appear during drying they will not show a garish white. Also, with top cover in place, plaster in its virgin state becomes difficult to paint. Try mixing very fine sand in the Polyfilla for a textured finish. Some PVA glue added to the mixture will help 'bind' it and produce a more durable ground cover.

Water

Making imitation water is surrounded by a lot of mystique. Most of this is unfounded, and modelling water is very easy to do in a scenic setting.

The easiest and most basic, yet still very convincing, method is varnish, correctly applied. All that's needed to represent running water are two or three coats of a good quality, clear polyurethane varnish, brushed on a previously painted surface, such as plaster, whether smooth or rough. The convincing touch lies in the colours that are painted on to represent the water. Remember, water isn't always, or rather doesn't always appear, blue! Again, environment is important and this should be considered in the planning stages.

Never use glass to represent water on dioramas that can be moved or held to be viewed. It may be fine for a fixed location but glass is dangerous and breaks easily, often with disastrous results on contact with human skin. Many modellers will insist on using glass when clear acrylic sheet (Perspex or Plexiglass) is available. Although more expensive than glass, acrylic is more adaptable and ripples can be formed on its surface with acrylic gel or liquid intended for using with paints. Acrylic can also be spaced over a stream or river bed for greater illusion of depth, and you can paint its undersurface for effect.

Clear castings resins are now used quite a lot to represent water and are very easy to mix and apply. All you need to ensure is that a natural barrier must be in place to stop the resin 'creeping' where it shouldn't. Resins will tend to 'creep' upwards on terrain which destroys any illusion, particularly on river banks. So, if possible, model the banks, dock walls or whatever *over* the edges of the resin. Alternatively, make the water off the diorama and add it as a one-piece moulding later. Form the area of water on a flat, but well-greased (Vaseline or any petroleum jelly will do) surface. When set, any surface tackiness can be removed with acetone – or use ladies' nail varnish remover.

For water with a choppy or rough surface, pour the resin onto slightly crumpled aluminium foil and proceed as for calm water, using the surface nearest the foil as the finished model. However, ensure that your waves are 'in scale' to the model; a choppy surface is required, not a line of individual 'tidal waves'.

Resins can be coloured, so there is plenty of scope here. Also, they can be 'layered', allowing each successive coat to dry, for depth and at each layer vegetation or such like added.

It's important that any plastic figures which are to be positioned in the water must be painted first, otherwise the resin could react with them and melt the plastic.

Grass

Grass, both long and short varieties, is found in practically every environment, from lush green to the scorched stubby variety.

For finely clipped, short grass the model hobby trade some years ago came up with a very good 'substitute' called 'static' or

Marcus Nicholls obtained a good water effect with laying acrylic medium on a varnished surface.

Left: tubs of static grass
from the German
manufacturer Noch.
Below: sheets of scenic
base material are ideal for
covering larger areas and
can be purchased in model
railway shops.

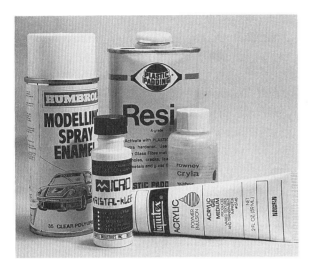

Readily available materials useful for producing water in vignettes and dioramas. Left to right: clear polyurethane varnish spray, 'Kristal-Kleer' glazing material, clear casting resin, tube of acrylic polymer emulsion and Rowney Cryla water tension breaker used with Rowney's Cryla Gloss.

Dried sawdust is still one of the cheapest and best texturing materials. It can be produced at home or bought in model railway shops.

Weathering powders, these are from Carr's, are available in all colours . . . even green and yellow as here. Their many uses will be limited only by the modeller's imagination.

'Streu' grass, or Noch, which is a trade name. Static grass consists of very fine individual nylon flock hairs, 2mm–3mm long. The material can be scattered evenly from a 'puffer pack' over a previously glued area – PVA glue is best because it dries transparent – and the excess is blown away, which causes the individual 'hairs' to stand erect. When all is completely dry, painting and toning down must be done, because as supplied, some static grass is a little gaudy in colour and can look unnatural over a large area.

Static grass is available already stuck down on brown paper sheets or in rolls to be glued down on flat surfaces. Gentle curves are possible but any bumpy terrain needs a little adjusting over the contours. Again, it needs painting to tone it down somewhat.

For 'clumps' of grass on the static grass areas, add some chopped dyed plastic cellular foam, universally referred to as 'foam rubber'. This material, available commercially, is very good for representing foliage also. It is on sale in model shops which stock scenic materials – usually for railway modellers, packed in plastic bags.

Long grass is a little more difficult to reproduce convincingly. Sisal or hemp rope or string are two good substitutes. The former must be boiled first to remove the size added during its manufacture, then stretched under weight before unwinding and cutting to manageable single-fibre lengths. Then it should be dyed a dark green, if required, using natural or chemical dyes obtainable from hardware stores.

Unwound ropes and strings provide the stalks of long grass which are 'inserted' into patches of PVA glue. Do not drill holes and push in clumps of the string, for nothing looks worse or less real. Work on small areas at a time if a large expanse is to be covered, and cover it bit-by-bit until all is in place. This way the grass will stand until the glue sets. When all is dry, trim with nail scissors for an even or uneven finish, blow off the surplus, then paint and dry brush for effect.

Medical lint sold in the chemists is a very useful material, in that its fluffy side can be used for making grass. Liberally coat the area to be covered with PVA glue and, while this is still tacky, press the lint, furry side down, onto it. When the glue has dried out, pull back the sheet of lint which should leave all the fibres adhering ready for trimming and painting. Experiment with small areas first.

Experiment with bristles from old brushes too, and always be on the lookout for new and not-so-obvious substitutes for grass.

Cromwell's A13 on the TV Models' plaster cast country lane base. The base is an ideal location for displaying and photographing model vehicles and figures.

Natural, dyed lichen material whilst widely used by modellers is a bit too limp for scenic work.

Hedgerows and Trees

Far too many modellers use far too much untreated natural and dyed lichen to represent trees and hedges on their models. Left untreated it looks . . . just like lichen!

If possible, leave lichen well alone; it's not cheap and there are better unnatural materials for scenic work now available on the market.

Rubberised horsehair (hair sprayed in a rubber solution and formed into honey-

Rubberised horsehair is easy to work and can be used for a basis of tree foliage and it makes very good hedges too.

Above: white metal tree trunks and cellular foam mat foliage from the American company Woodland Scenics. *Below*: etched brass leaves when used correctly for scenic work can look most convincing.

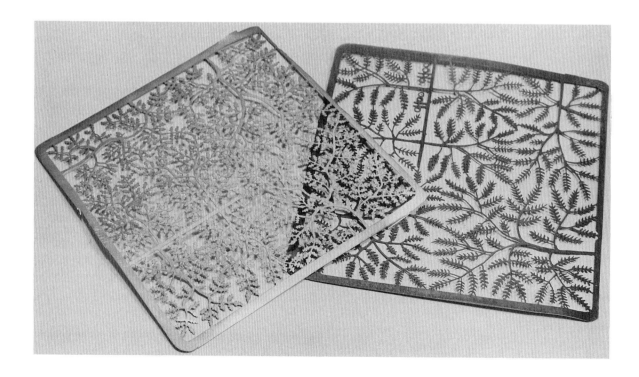

A tree kit from Scale Link (right) using cast white metal trunks and rubberised horsehair foliage. To the left is another system using plastic fork-shaped trunks for smaller scale trees.

combed 'blocks', as used by upholsterers, is cheap and easy to work with. Finished with shredded dyed foam foliage, a good hedge, bush or tree results. All can be stuck together with PVA glue. Suitable natural twigs are easily adapted and pressed into service as tree trunks and branches or as bare trees, such as those found in winter. Keep your eyes open for any likely examples when you're out walking in the country or when taking a stroll around the garden at home.

Fine multi-strand wire rope unwound to form trunk and branches is worth investigating. Use gloves when you handle it, however, otherwise it is easy to cut or puncture the skin on your hands. Once the shape is decided upon, coat with either epoxy glue or solder then skim with plaster or epoxy filler to model the bark details. Paint black and then colour and dry brush for a realistic appearance.

Foliage can either be rubberised horsehair and dyed foam stuck on or, as marketed by the US company, Woodland Scenics, an open weave mat that can be 'teased' out to shape to form foliage. White metal trunks, branches and foliage are available in the Scale Link Company's range of scenic accessories. This company also makes photo-etched leaves and other vegetation. These are expensive but many modellers use them to effect, though, without careful handling and positioning, they can look a little 'mechanical'.

Remember, a mature tree is big. This should be borne in mind when a diorama is planned. A fully matured oak in 54mm scale would be massive and not really practical for a diorama – the tree would dominate at the expense of everything else. Some form of compromise is needed.

Also, get your areas correct. The desert-type date palm tree is different from the lofty coconut South Seas palm that some modellers place incorrectly over their German WW2 *Afrika Korps* tanks! Refer to pictures whenever possible.

Special Effects

Finally, a word about snow, a medium which seems to find great favour amongst beginners, especially.

Model snow as an overall cover can look quite good, just as a light 'powdering' of snow can look extremely effective too. Model the stuff in plaster and paint it white, but also allow some groundwork to show here and there simply for relief of monotony if the expanse of ground is great. Wherever ridges are formed, run some salt and powdered alum (available from chemists) on these for a little light reflection of the crystals. Don't use sugar because its grains are too coarse and it dissolves fairly easily and quickly to a syrup-like mass after contact with water-based paints and glues, thus losing its sparkle. Light applications of snow can be made with baking soda.

Icicles look good on buildings and structures in winter dioramas, and can be made by heat-stretching acrylic rod (ABS Plastruct range) of the clear variety and texturing it with acrylic medium to obtain a smooth glassy surface, then varnishing to finish. Again, although massive icicles are often found, don't let them overpower any scene you're creating and play down their appearance as a feature.

Ice on water is best made with polyurethane varnish over a white-painted surface with a bluish tinge introduced at the edges, over which should be powdered a little 'snow' made up from baking soda. Snow and ice do not have a matt finish; they shine because of the effects of light falling on crystallised water, so try to make your diorama 'twinkle' here and there, but don't overdo it to distraction.

Dioramas are an adventure in themselves, and should be explored fully by military modellers who should look upon them as an extension of building a single vehicle or painting a figure. When you think about it, it's a lot more fun and more satisfying to incorporate your modelling skills and output into a miniature scenic setting that perhaps represents a true event from history or the result of your own imagination coming to fruition.

Hecker and Goros figures, a Prussian and Bavarian, in a snowy scenic setting.

APPENDICES

USEFUL ADDRESSES – MANUFACTURERS, MUSEUMS, SOCIETIES . . .

Accurate Armour Ltd
Unit 16, Ardgowan Street Industrial Estate, Port Glasgow, Scotland PA14 5DG

Resin vehicle kits; 1:35 scale

Almond Sculptures Ltd
The Nook, Fawsett Hill, Lower Hardres, Canterbury, Kent CT4 7AJ

Miniature figurine kits 90mm

Andrea Miniatures
Josefa Diaz 12, 28038 Madrid, Spain

Miniature figurine kits scales varied; mainly 54mm and 90mm

Azimut
19 rue Saint Jacques, 38000 Grenoble, France

Resin vehicle kits; 1:35 scale

Airmodel
Frank Modellbau, Obere Vorstadt 21, D–7470, Albstadt 1, Germany

Vacuum-formed plastic vehicle kits

Julian Benassi
55 St Mungo Avenue, Glasgow, Scotland G4 0PL

Miniature figurine kits; scales various

Border Miniatures
Fernlea, Chestnut Hill, Keswick, Cumbria CA12 4PB

Miniature figurine kits and accessories; mainly 80mm scale

Chota Sahib
124 Springfield Road, Brighton, Sussex BN1 6DE

Miniature figurine kits; mainly 54mm scale

Clydecast Products
97 Fereneze Avenue, Clarkston, Glasgow, Scotland G76 7RT

Miniature figurine kits; 75mm and 90mm scales

Continental Model Supply Co
36 Gray Gardens, Rainham, Essex, RM13 7NH

Miniature military vehicles; 1:76 and 1:87 scales (Minitanks)

Carr's Modelling Products
Unit 5, Centre 88 Elm Grove, Wimbledon, London SW19 4HE

Soldering equipment, weathering powders and varied accessories

Craft Supplies
Millers Dale, Buxton, Derby SK17 8SN

Glass domes, etc.

J.B. Church
Honeywood, Middle Road, Tiptoe, Nr. Lymington, Hants. SO4 0FX

Military vehicle scale plans

Trevor Claringbold
18 Bevan Way, Aylesham, Kent CT3 3DN

Military vehicle scale plans

Cromwell Models
Regency House, 22 Hayburn Street, Partick, Glasgow G11 6DG

Resin vehicle kits; 1:76 and 1:35 scale

Daylight Studios
223a Portobello Road, London W11 1LU

Lamps and blue daylight bulbs for accurate colour matching

Ensign Miniatures
Littlebury Hall, Station Road, Kirton, Lincs PE20 1LG

Miniature figurine kits; mainly 54mm

Elastolin (Preiser Germany)
Gaugemaster Controls, Gaugemaster House, Ford Road, Arundel, W. Sussex BN18 0BN

Plastic figures

D.F. Grieve Models
St. Andrews, Westwood Road, Betsham, Nr. Gravesend, Kent DA13 9LZ

Miniature figurine kits; mainly 100mm

Historex Agents
3 Castle Street, Dover, Kent CT16 1QJ

Miniature figurines, vehicle kits and modelling accessories. UK agents for the French Historex range of plastic figure kits, which at the time of writing has gone into 'Judicial Receivership' in Paris.

Hornet Models
PO Box 64, Rochester, Kent ME1 3JR

Miniature figurine kits 1:35 scale

W.E. Hersant Ltd
228 Archway Road, London N6 5AZ

Specialist military booksellers

Humbrol Ltd
Marfleet, Hull HU9 5NE

Paints, construction kits and accessories

Harrow Model Shop
190–194 Station Road, Harrow, Middlesex

Stockists of figure and vehicle kits and accessories

W. Hobby Ltd
Knights Hill Square, London SE27 0HH

Modellers' tools and accessories

Richard Kohnstam
13/15 High Street, Hemel Hempstead, Herts

Importers of Tamiya, Dragon and Italeri plastic construction kits

Langley Models
166 Three Bridges Road, Crawley, Sussex RH10 1LE

Miniature figurines and accessories

Lead Sled Models
Unit 3, Round House Craft Centre, Buckland-in-the-Moor, Ashburton, Devon TQ13 7HN

Military vehicle and figure kits

Mitrecap Miniatures
Manorfield Galleries, Manorfield House, Main Street, Aston-cum-Augton, Sheffield S31 0XJ

Miniature figures; scales various

Milicast Glasgow
990 Pollokshaws Road, Shawlands, Glasgow G41 2HA

Military vehicle kits 1:76 scale

Mil Art
120 Ashley Road, Dover Court, Harwich,
Essex CO12 4AR

Miniature figurine kits; scales various

Milliput Company
Unit 5, Marian Mawr Industrial Estate,
Dolgellau, Gwynedd, Wales

Manufacturer of epoxy putties

MMS
26 Crescent Rise, Luton, Beds LU2 0AU

Military vehicle kits; 1:76 scale

Morgan Book Services
84 Bushwood Road, Kew Gardens, Surrey
TW9 3BQ

Specialist military books

New Hope Design
Rijksweg 42, 6269 AC Margraten, The
Netherlands

*Miniature figurine kits; mainly 54mm
scale*

Ostmodels
8 Kingswood Crescent, Berridale 7011,
Tasmania, Australia

Military vehicle kits; 1:76 scale

Poste Militaire
Station Road, Northiam, Rye, East Sussex
TN31 6QT

Miniature figurine kits; mainly 90mm

J. Peddinghaus
Beethovenstrasse 20, 5870 Hemer,
Germany

Figurines, vehicle kits and accessories

Phoenix Model Developments Ltd
The Square, Earls Barton, Northampton
NN6 0NA

*Miniature figurine kits and accessories;
scales various*

Positive Figurines
52 Donellan Green, Southfields, Northampton NN3 5DJ

Miniature figurine kits; scales various

Pompadour Gallery
Fairview Parade, Mawnay Road, Romford,
Essex

Postcards

Plaka
G.H. Smith & Partners Ltd., Berechurch
Road, Colchester, Essex CO2 7QH

Plaka paints (UK)

Proops
Unit E, New Crescent Works, 3 Nicoll
Road, London NW 10 9AX

*Miniature tools and accessories for the
modeller*

Plastruct Inc
1020 S. Wallace Place Industry, CA 91748
USA

ABS plastic construction materials

Punctilio Model Spot
Waterloo Road, Rugby Road Corner,
Hinckley, Leics LE10 0QJ

*Items for the modeller including stocks of
Rose Paints*

Southford Products
31 Ely Close, South Minster, Essex
CM0 7AQ

*Metal products – paint boxes and turn-
tables*

Sovereign
John Tassell, 4 Hawbeck Road, Rainham, Gillingham, Kent

Figurine and vehicle kits

Skytrex Ltd
Unit 3, Canal Bank, Loughborough, Leicestershire

Vehicle and figure kits

Scale Link Co
178 High Street, Teddington, Middlesex TW11 8HU

Vehicle and figure kits – First World War

Scorpio
20 Ordnance Row, The Hard, Portsmouth, Hants PO1 3DN

Figurine kit stockist

S & S Models
3 Dewer Close, Burnham-on-Sea, Sussex

Vehicle kits

Brian Sherriff Ltd
35 Cowgate, Dundee, Scotland DD1 2LW

Major stockist – large range of kits, figures, accessories

Squadron Signal Publications Inc
1115 Crowley Drive, Carrollton, Texas 75011–5010 USA

Specialist military book publishers and model shops

Tradition
5a Shepherd Street, Mayfair, London W1

Miniature figurine stockist

Alec Tiranti Ltd
70 High Street, Theale, Reading, Berks

Moulding rubbers, resins, metals and accessories for modellers

Tomker Models
Verbondstraat 68, 2000 Antwerpen, Belgium

Miniature figurine kits

Thistle Miniatures
Findon Croft, Findon, Aberdeen, Scotland AB1 4RN

Miniature figurine kits

Tiny Troopers (Mike French Models)
19 Langton Road, Boscombe, Bournemouth, Dorset BH7 6HS

Miniature figurine kits

The Trumpet Banner
88a Sandgate High Street, Folkestone, Kent CT20 3BY

Miniature figurine kit stockist

T.V. Models
147 Faulds Gate, Aberdeen, Scotland AB1 5RB

Miniature figurine kits and scenic accessories

Verlinden Productions
Ondernemersstraat 4, KMO Zone Mallekot, 8–2500 Lier, Belgium (Verlinden, Letterman and Stok 25 Cross Keys Center Florissant, MO 63033, USA)

Miniature figurine kits, vehicles and scenic accessories

MUSEUMS AND SOCIETIES

Museum of Army Transport
Flemingate, Beverley, North Humberside

Collection of military vehicles

British Model Soldier Society
Secretary – David Pierce, 22 Lynwood Drive, Ealing, London W5 1JJ

Imperial War Museum
Lambeth Road, London SE1 and Duxford
Airfield, Cambridgeshire

International Plastic Modellers Society
Membership – J. Wright, 9 Pretoria Road,
Gillingham, Kent ME7 4ND

International Plastic Modellers Society USA
PO Box 6369, Lincoln, NE 68506, USA.

Irish Model Soldier Society
Secretary – Liam Whelan, 56 The Grove,
Celbridge, Co. Kildare, Eire

Miniature Armoured Fighting Vehicle Association
G.E.G. Williams, 15 Berwick Avenue,
Stockport, Cheshire SK4 3AA

National Army Museum
Royal Hospital Road, Chelsea, London
SW3 4HT

Patton Museum of Cavalry and Armour
PO Box 208, Fort Knox, KY 40121–0208,
USA

Scottish Military Collectors Society
Secretary – James B. McKay, 17/14 St.
Andrew's Crescent, Pollockshields,
Glasgow, Scotland G41 5SH

The Tank Museum
Bovington Camp, Wareham, Dorset BN20
6JG

APPENDIX 2
MAGAZINES

Modelling and non-modelling titles with a direct interest

After the Battle
After the Battle Publications
Church House, Church Street, London E15 3JA

Fine Scale Modeller
Kalmbach Publishing Co., 21027 Crossroads Circle, PO Box 1612, Waukesha WI 53187 USA

In Scale
Traplet House, Severn Drive, Upton-on-Severn, Worcs WR8 0JL

Military Hobbies
Pireme Publishing Ltd., 34 Chatsworth Road, Charminster, Bournemouth, Dorset BH8 8SW

Military Illustrated
43 Museum Street, London WC1A 1LY

Military Modelling
Argus House, Boundary Way, Hemel Hempstead, Herts HP2 7ST

Model Art International
84 Victoria Road, Swindon, Wilts SN1 3BB

Model Graphix
Artbox, Fuji Green Mansion 301, 19 Nakamachi, Shinjuku-ku, Tokyo, Japan 162

Scale Models International
Argus House, Boundary Way, Hemel Hempstead, Herts HP2 7ST

Tamiya Magazine
Argus House, Boundary Way, Hemel Hempstead, HP2 7ST

Verlinden Publications
Ondernmersstraat 4, KMO-Zone Mallekot, 8–2500 Lier, Belgium

APPENDIX 3
RECOMMENDED BOOKS FOR THE MILITARY MODELLER

At the time of writing some of the books listed may be out of print. However, the public library system and specialist second-hand book dealers who advertise in the model press can usually obtain titles to order.

The Verlinden Way – Vols I – V, Francois Verlinden
Ondernemersstraat 4, KMO-Zone Mallekot, 8–2500 Lier, Belgium

The Modelmaker's Handbook – Albert Jackson & David Day ISBN 0–07207–1250–5
Pelham Books, 44 Bedford Square, London WC1B 3DU

Modelling Military Vehicles – Bill Evans & David Parker ISBN 0–7090–4021–0
Robert Hale Ltd., 45–47 Clerkenwell Green, London EC1R 0HT

How to Build Dioramas – Sheperd Paine ISBN 0–89024–551–7
Kalmbach Publishing Co., 1027 North Seventh Street, Milwaukee, WI 53233 USA

Modeling Tanks and Military Vehicles – Sheperd Paine ISBN 0–89024–045–0
Kalmbach Publishing Co., 1027 North Seventh Street, Milwaukee, WI 53233 USA

How to Photograph Scale Models – Sheperd Paine and Lane Stewart ISBN 0–89024–053–1
Kalmbach Publishing Co., 1027 North Seventh Street, Milwaukee, WI 53233 USA

The Art of the Diorama – Ray Anderson ISBN 0–89024–092–2
Kalmbach Publishing Co., 1027 North Seventh Street, Milwaukee, WI 53233 USA

INDEX

INDEX

NOTES